Coaching in Gifted Education

Gifted students spend most of their time in the regular classroom, yet few general education teachers have the specialized training to address their unique needs. This book provides the structures, processes, and resources needed to facilitate GT (Gifted/Talented) coaching as a means of building capacity among classroom teachers to identify, serve, and teach gifted and high-potential learners.

Guided by best practices and research in professional learning, this resource provides the steps, strategies, and tools needed to create and sustain effective coaching practices designed to maximize access to advanced learning and differentiation throughout a school. Bolstered by downloadable resources, chapters address how to support, stretch, and sustain teachers' instructional practices through a sequence of co-thinking, co-planning, and reflection that emphasizes ongoing and sustainable professional learning.

Outlining a step-by-step guide for the coaching process, this valuable resource equips gifted and talented coaches with tools to support teachers to meet the needs and reveal talent among gifted and high-potential students through differentiation in the regular education classroom.

Emily Mofield, Ed.D. is an Assistant Professor in the College of Education at Lipscomb University, USA. She has over 20 years of experience in the field of gifted education as a teacher, district leader, researcher, assistant professor, consultant, and author, also serving as curriculum studies chair for NAGC.

Vicki Phelps, Ed.D. is Head of School for Quest Academy, a school for gifted learners, in Palatine, IL, USA. She has been involved in gifted education for over 25 years, including teaching and leading gifted services, serving as an assistant professor, working as a gifted consultant, and serving as special schools and programs chair for NAGC.

Coaching in Gifted Education

Tools for Building Capacity and Catalyzing Change

Emily Mofield
& Vicki Phelps

Routledge
Taylor & Francis Group

NEW YORK AND LONDON

Cover image: © Getty Images

First published 2024
by Routledge
605 Third Avenue, New York, NY 10158

and by Routledge
4 Park Square, Milton Park, Abingdon, Oxon, OX14 4RN

Routledge is an imprint of the Taylor & Francis Group, an informa business

© 2024 Taylor & Francis

Library of Congress Cataloging-in-Publication Data
Names: Mofield, Emily, 1979– author. | Phelps, Vicki, author.
Title: Coaching in gifted education : tools for building capacity and catalyzing change/Emily Mofield &
    Vicki Phelps.
Description: New York, NY : Routledge, 2024. | Includes bibliographical references. | Summary:—Provided by
    publisher.
Identifiers: LCCN 2022059875 (print) | LCCN 2022059876 (ebook) | ISBN 9781032375151 (hardback) |
    ISBN 9781032375144 (paperback) | ISBN 9781003340560 (ebook)
Subjects: LCSH: Gifted children—Education. | Motivation in education. | Gifted children—Education—
    Curricula. | Individualized instruction.
Classification: LCC LC3993 .M63 2024 (print) | LCC LC3993 (ebook) | DDC 371.95/6—dc23/eng/20221216
LC record available at https://lccn.loc.gov/2022059875
LC ebook record available at https://lccn.loc.gov/2022059876

ISBN: 978-1-032-37515-1 (hbk)
ISBN: 978-1-032-37514-4 (pbk)
ISBN: 978-1-003-34056-0 (ebk)

DOI: 10.4324/9781003340560

Typeset in Warnock Pro
by Apex CoVantage, LLC

Access the Support Material: www.routledge.com/9781032375144

Dedication

To my forever best friend, soulmate, husband, Ashley Mofield- for always loving, supporting, cheering, and encouraging me. To Ellie – you are my ray of sunshine!

—Emily

Soli deo gloria

To my beloved husband, David – your ability to help me reflect, navigate, and celebrate life is more than I could ask for. To my children, Brittany, Becca, and David- the greatest parts of me are a result of you.

—Vicki

Soli deo gloria

Contents

List of Resources

Acknowledgements

We would like to acknowledge the educators, instructional coaches, and leaders who have shared invaluable feedback on the GT Coaching Circuit. We want to especially thank Tina Moore and Zenobia Denney for allowing us a space to field test many of these ideas and know next steps for fine-tuning the processes involved in GT Coaching. We also appreciate the Ayers Institute and the Catalyst Coaching initiative of Lipscomb University for providing a solid foundation for thinking about coaching as building capacity in others for catalyzing change.

Introduction

The purpose of this resource is to provide the structures, processes, and resources needed to facilitate GT (Gifted/Talented) coaching. GT coaching builds capacity among classroom teachers to identify, serve, and teach gifted and high-potential learners. Gifted students spend most of their time in the regular classroom, yet few general education teachers have specialized training to address the needs of gifted students. Coaching allows for the ongoing professional learning for teachers, where they receive personalized feedback and use reflection as a means for changing beliefs, behaviors, and practices in the classroom. This resource equips GT coaches with tools for fostering collaborative relationships and provides the steps, strategies, and tools needed to create and sustain effective coaching practices aimed to maximize access to advanced learning and differentiation throughout a school.

In 2020, we co-authored *Collaboration, Coteaching, and Coaching: Sharing Strategies to Support Gifted Learners* (Mofield & Phelps, 2020). We were thrilled to see how teachers responded to this resource and how they applied many of the core principles of collaboration to their daily practices. That book included one chapter on instructional coaching applied to gifted education contexts. Since its release, we have continued to grow in our understanding of this dynamic, reflective process of leading change. We have learned so much more about the promise of coaching in the field of gifted education and the need to create a practical structure for a coaching sequence, especially since

DOI: 10.4324/9781003340560-1

many districts have expanded the role of the gifted education teacher to that of a "differentiation" or "enrichment" coach. This endeavor included studying the underlying principles behind coaching models that already exist in education including cognitive coaching (Costa & Garmston, 2015; Kee et al., 2010), instructional coaching (Knight, 2018), content-based coaching (West, 2019), and transformational coaching (Aguilar, 2013).

We learned that many leaders and teachers were seeking to determine what instructional coaching might look like in contexts of gifted education. We found that even though there are numerous coaching books in education, many offer only conceptual perspectives (the "why" of coaching) without concrete direction on *how* to serve as a coach. Other times we felt that the coaching literature focused on coaches guiding a teacher to think about what they already know within their instructional toolbox, but in the context of supporting classroom teachers in differentiation, there is often a gap in knowledge or awareness of how to serve gifted/high-potential populations.

This led to our design of the GT Coaching Circuit. Throughout this book, we present this as a map for moving through a coaching sequence. While we do not believe that our coaching model is the "only" or "right" way to implement coaching to identify, serve, and teach gifted and high-potential students, we do believe it provides a practical, flexible framework for GT coaches, based on foundational principles in the coaching field. We share *why* coaching leads to lasting buy-in and changing practices, *what* the role of a GT coach entails, and describe a step-by-step process for *how* to engage teachers through a coaching sequence for growth and reflection. We also include example scenarios, guides with question prompts, and a variety of tools to equip GT coaches for success.

We believe that coaching in gifted education is also an opportunity for the field to address issues of equity, align goals with other district initiatives, and promote meaningful change. Additionally, coaching paves the way for building a climate of collective capacity within a school and district where teachers understand their role in supporting all learners (including gifted students). Therefore, this book also provides insight into best practices for coaching and building collective capacity to drive shared decision-making at the classroom, school, and district level.

Does Coaching Work?

Coaching is a powerful approach to professional learning because it is ongoing in nature. The typical one time "sit and get" training on gifted characteristics and differentiated instruction often offered to classroom teachers is not likely to stick. Classic research on professional development suggests that teachers only transfer 5–25% of what they learn in training that includes explanation of theory, demonstration, and practice (Joyce et al., 1987). However, long-term application of learning increases to 90% when coaching is added to professional development as follow-through. Additionally, recent meta-analyses have shown positive effects of coaching on teacher instruction, ranging in effect sizes from .47 (i.e., coaching of general practices) to .51 (i.e., content-specific coaching) (Kraft et al., 2018). These effect sizes are considered moderate, but also impressive given the number of variables that can potentially affect teacher instruction.

Coaching is also noted to be a major factor for sustainable professional learning. Darling-Hammond et al. (2017) noted through a meta-analysis of over 35 studies that effective professional learning is content-focused, includes active learning, involves collaboration, uses effective models, provides coaching and expert support, allows for feedback and reflection, and is of sustained duration. Though coaching itself is one of these seven features, it is important to note that it is largely connected to the others. Coaching allows for the follow-up of professional learning in the teacher's own classroom setting (including content-based application, active learning, feedback, reflection, etc.).

Professional Learning Standards

Coaching in gifted education aligns to professional standards in Professional Learning. For example, the NAGC (2019) Gifted Programming Standards emphasize the ongoing reflective nature of coaching in the following standards:

- ¬ 6.4.1. Educators regularly reflect on and assess their instructional practices, develop professional learning plans, and improve their practices by participating in continuing education opportunities.
- ¬ 6.4.2. Educators participate in professional learning that is sustained over time, incorporates collaboration and reflection, is goal-aligned and data driven, is coherent, embedded and transferable, includes regular follow-up, and seeks evidence of positive impact on teacher practice and on increased student learning.

Additionally, the World Council for Gifted and Talented Children (WCGTC, 2021) has adopted 10 Global Principles for Professional Learning. These principles emphasize *ongoing* and *sustainable* professional learning:

- + *Ongoing.* A professional learning plan in gifted education should provide ongoing opportunities to refine and extend existing knowledge and skills through in-service programs and other professional learning experiences throughout a career.

+ *Sustainable.* Professional learning in gifted education should be built into educational policy of the state, region, province and/or country. Programs should be monitored regularly, and accountability systems should be in place. Collaboration between all stakeholders – policymakers, school authorities, community members, higher education faculty, and others – is actively encouraged (WCGTC, 2021, p. 3).

Coaching, indeed, allows for regular follow-up opportunities for teachers to reflect on how their decisions impact student learning and is one part of a multi-part system for promoting sustainable change.

Theoretical Foundations

The work of coaching has conceptual foundations in self-efficacy theory and constructivism. Teacher self-efficacy, the belief in one's ability to influence student learning, is shown to have an impact on teacher effectiveness and student learning (Klassen & Tze, 2014). Therefore, a key question is, what produces teacher self-efficacy? According to self-efficacy theory (Bandura, 1997), there are four sources that play a role: mastery experiences, vicarious experiences, verbal persuasion, and affective states. Relevant to this book, each one of these factors can be developed through a coaching partnership. Teachers grow in their abilities to use an instructional strategy (i.e., mastery experience), they see other teachers or the coach model a strategy so they believe they, too, can apply it (i.e., vicarious experience), they experience encouraging, positive interactions throughout the coaching process (i.e., verbal persuasion), and they work through emotional arousal (e.g., stress) from dialogue with a coach or experience positive emotion (i.e., affective states) from the coaching interaction. Studies have linked these four sources of efficacy to coaching in school contexts (e.g., Bowman et al., 2021) finding positive results for teachers and student outcomes. When teachers gain confidence in their abilities to affect student learning through the coaching process, they do, indeed, impact student learning.

Coaching, like other forms of collaborative inquiry, is also rooted in constructivist theory. You will see throughout this book that we emphasize coaching is not "advice-giving." Instead, it is an interaction of ideas between co-thinking partners. When the teacher and coach come together in a reflective process, they construct new knowledge (Shakenova, 2017). This interaction of ideas and decision-making leads to new possibilities and learning where the coach serves a conduit of thinking. Knight (2020) noted, "When we help a teacher think, we help them create." This is ultimately what coaching is all about-guiding teacher thinking to create new opportunities for students to learn and thrive.

The Impact of Coaching in Gifted Education

As far as how coaching is applied to gifted education, we know of only a handful of studies that have examined its outcomes. Peer-coaching has shown positive effects for supporting the growth of administrators' knowledge and skills regarding gifted students (Cotabish & Robinson, 2012). Also, in a case study, Tieso (2004) found that through the use of peer coach study teams, teachers used more differentiation in their classrooms and students perceived more opportunities to work at their own pace and in their own areas of interest. In another study, the use of peer-coaching/mentoring was noted to have positive impacts on the use of differentiation practices for high-ability students, though a number of challenges surfaced such as scheduling logistics and communication about the roles of peer-coaches/mentors (Latz et al., 2009).

We have field-tested elements of our GT Coaching Circuit in a few school districts across the nation, though we are just now beginning the process of collecting formal data. We have received input from a number of teachers and coaches on its structure and application within schools. Additionally, gifted coordinators and educational coaches have reviewed the model and provided valuable feedback on its components and organization. We are deeply appreciative of the feedback and suggestions for revision on this model.

In the development of the GT Coaching Circuit, we also borrowed heavily from what we know about effective literacy coaching. For example, the literature suggests using a combination of the following three approaches to build buy-in among teachers: leverage relationships, build efficacy through explicit demonstration of the instructional intervention (process), and link teacher actions to student outcomes (results) (Cutrer, 2016). You will notice that these are adapted for GT contexts and are embedded throughout the GT Coaching Circuit intentionally.

What to Expect in the Pages Ahead

The focus of this book is to provide a rationale for coaching as applied to gifted education and outline a step-by-step guide for the coaching process. We should point out that this book is not a book of instructional strategies to share with teachers; rather, it is a book of how to coach teachers to learn and reflect on the impact of instructional strategies on student learning. While we do describe a few instructional strategies (see Appendix C for a list of our recommended resources), we focus more on the *process* of coaching teachers through ongoing dialogue and reflection.

We also acknowledge coaching overlaps with the collaborative teaching practices such as co-planning or even co-teaching. This book, however, does not address those collaborative teaching practices in detail (our other book, *Collaboration, Coteaching, and Coaching in Gifted Education: Sharing Strategies to Support Gifted Learners* [Mofield & Phelps, 2020] does so).

The book is outlined as follows:

+ Chapter 1 provides a rationale for coaching in gifted education - to build capacity in other teachers to identify, serve, and teach gifted students. We present the rationale through the lens of talent development and introduce a framework for coaching through TEAM (Trust, Engage others' Expertise, Align, and Maintain).

+ Chapter 2 describes the role of a GT coach. We describe the guiding beliefs of a coach (i.e., the coach's mindset), a lens for thinking about relationships with others, and how core values shape beliefs and actions. We share key considerations of structures needed to pave the way for successful GT coaching.

+ Chapter 3 describes skills for communicating in coaching conversations. We describe committed listening, paraphrasing, using reflective feedback, and responding to teachers who resist coaching.

+ Chapter 4 introduces the first stage of the GT Coaching Circuit – Set a Purpose. This stage includes evaluate the need, establish a goal, and explore options.

+ Chapter 5 provides an overview of the second stage of the GT Coaching Circuit – Plan and Act. This stage includes supporting a teacher in selecting a strategy and learning how to use the strategy. A strategy is selected by considering differentiation features, alignment to the teacher's purpose, and application to the teacher's specific context. Teachers grow in their capacity to use the strategy through modeling, co-planning, or co-teaching with the coach.

+ Chapter 6 outlines the third stage of the GT Coaching Circuit – Reflect. Within this stage, teachers reflect on goal attainment, reflect on the process of growth, and reflect forward to next steps. In doing so, teachers examine how their own efficacy has evolved throughout the coaching process and engage in metacognitive reflection as a means to engage in the transfer of learning to future instructional practice.

+ Chapter 7 describes how to make a plan for GT coaching visible, defensible, and sustainable by developing a shared vision with administrators. We discuss the importance of aligning aims with other school-based goals, leveraging collective efficacy, working with PLCs or other school-based teams, and using GT coaching as a means towards promoting equity in identifying and serving students from underrepresented groups.

As you dive into this work of GT coaching, know this resource is only a starting point for deep interpersonal work. Working with other human beings can be complex as we all have different values, beliefs, and assumptions about learning and teaching. Though coaching can be a challenging endeavor, we hope to provide a rationale and structure for paving the way to facilitate its possibilities for student success. We believe there is important work to be done in the field of gifted education, particularly in how to equitably provide services to meet the needs and reveal talent among gifted and high-potential students through differentiation in the regular education classroom. GT coaching is one way to catalyze this change and support students to understand, show, and grow their gifts and talents.

References

Aguilar, E. (2013). The art of coaching: *Effective strategies for school transformation*. Wiley.

Bandura, A. (1997). *Self-efficacy: The exercise of control*. W. H. Freeman/Times Books/ Henry Holt & Co.

Bowman, E., Hamilton, B., & Pratt, A. (2021). *A mixed-methods study on the perceived quality and impact of professional development on urban school district educators* (Publication No. 28644701) [Doctoral Dissertation, Lipscomb University]. ProQuest Dissertations and Theses Global.

Costa, A. L., & Garmston, R. J. (2015). *Cognitive coaching: Developing self-directed leaders and learners* (3rd ed.). Rowman & Littlefield.

Cotabish, A., & Robinson, A. (2012). The effects of peer coaching on the evaluation knowledge, skills, and concerns of gifted program administrators. *Gifted Child Quarterly*, *62*(3), 160–170. https://doi.org/10.1177/0016986212446861.

Cutrer, E. (2016). *The benefit of literacy coaching for initial resistance to implementation of a literacy program for struggling readers* (Doctoral dissertation). https://doi.org/10.17615/smjb-gq92.

Joyce, B., Showers, B., & Rolneiser-Bennett, C. (1987). Staff development and student learning: A synthesis of research on models of teaching. *Educational Leadership, 45*(2), 11–23.

Kee, K., Anderson, K., Dearing, V., Harris, E., & Shuster, F. (2010). *Results coaching: The new essentials for school leaders.* Corwin.

Klassen R. M., & Tze, V. M. C. (2014). Teachers' self-efficacy, personality, and teaching effectiveness: a meta-analysis. *Educational Research Review, 12,* 59–76. https://doi.org/10.1016/j.edurev.2014.06.001.

Knight, J. (2018). *The impact cycle: What instructional coaches should do to foster powerful improvements in teaching.* Corwin.

Knight, J. (2020, September 24). Instructional coaching with Jim Knight with Kim Richardson [Audio podcast]. Instructional Coaching Group. https://www.youtube.com/watch?v=DsXq13VrINc&feature=youtu.be.

Kraft, M. A., Blazar, D., & Hogan, D. (2018). The effect of teacher coaching on instruction and achievement: A meta-analysis of the causal evidence. *Review of Educational Research, 88*(4), 547–588. https://doi.org/10.3102/0034654318759268.

Latz, A. O., Speirs Neumeister, K. L., Adams, C. M., & Pierce, R. L. (2009). Peer coaching to improve classroom differentiation: Perspectives from project CLUE. *Roeper Review, 31*(1), 27–39. https://doi.org/10.1080/02783190802527356.

Mofield, E., & Phelps, V. (2020). *Collaboration, coteaching, and coaching in gifted education: Sharing strategies to support gifted learners.* Prufrock Press.

National Association for Gifted Children. (2019). *Pre-K–Grade 12 gifted programming standards.* http://www.nagc.org/sites/default/files/standards/Intro%202019%20Programming%20Standards.pdf.

Shakenova, L. (2017). The theoretical framework of teacher collaboration. *Khazar Journal of Humanities and Social Sciences, 20*(2), 34–48. https://doi.org/10.5782/2223-2621.2017.20.2.34.

Tieso, C. (2004). Through the looking glass: One school's reflections on differentiation. *Gifted Child Today, 27*(4): 58–65. https://doi.org/10.4219/gct-2004-155.

West, L. (2009). Content coaching: Transforming the teaching profession. In J. Knight (Ed.), *Coaching approaches and perspectives* (pp. 145–165). Corwin.

World Council for Gifted and Talented Children. (2021). *Global principles for professional learning in gifted education.* https://world-gifted.org/professional-learning-global-principles.pdf.

Chapter 1

Coaching as a Catalyst for Change

If you are reading this book, you are likely invested in answering this question, "How might we better identify, teach, and support gifted and high-potential students?" In order to know how to achieve this goal, we need to understand where we are in relation to it. Let's do a reality check. Many gifted students are taught in mixed-ability classrooms. Let's suppose a gifted student attends pull-out gifted instruction 2 hours per week. In a given 35-hour school week, this is only 6% of instructional time. As we know, gifted students are not just gifted on Tuesdays and Thursdays for a total of two hours. What is happening the remaining 32 hours of the week? Are the students appropriately challenged? Are students able to grow academically and progress in their learning?

In an ideal situation, gifted students receive some form of differentiated instruction in the regular education classroom, with modified tasks provided to elicit interest and challenge. However, classroom teachers often do not have training or developed skills to serve gifted students. Further, in today's educational climate, teachers are faced with a number of barriers to differentiation including mandated curriculum, pressures to focus on bringing students of low-proficiency levels to grade-level, and simply not having the time, energy, or resources to prepare materials.

DOI: 10.4324/9781003340560-2

Other barriers relate to belief systems. For example, Dixon et al. (2014) noted, "Teachers who have a one-size fits all attitude or cannot see the big picture of why this is needed, often do not think they can accomplish this process" (p. 123). Additionally, professional learning addressing the needs of gifted students is often limited. Callahan et al. (2014) found that among over 1500 schools surveyed, many only provided 15 minutes of professional development focused on providing services for gifted students. Though differentiation is touted as a proactive approach to responding to student differences, the reality is that more often than not, gifted students do not receive qualitatively different learning experiences to support their academic growth.

Now, let's consider the realities faced by GT teachers. In many districts GT teachers are spread thin across multiple schools. Many handle large caseloads, navigate complex schedules, write and revise individual gifted education plans, and facilitate collaboration with multiple stakeholders. Though we do believe that GT teachers are a bit super-human, we must admit that the GT teacher cannot "do it all" in terms of testing, teaching, advocating, and meeting the needs of gifted students. So, we must revise our original question to, "How, then, do we *build capacity in others* to identify, teach, and support gifted and high potential students?"

This is what coaching is all about. Coaching provides opportunities to create buy-in and share the ownership of serving gifted students. Coaching is also a form of professional learning that leads to sustainable practices, as opposed to offering mere "one and done, sit and get" in-services that are forgotten about a week or two later. While many classroom teachers might attend professional learning about strategies to challenge gifted students, research shows that only 20% of practices are implemented after such training, but with coaching, about 80–90% of practices are implemented (Joyce et al., 1987; Knight, 2007). Coaching allows for ongoing professional learning where teachers receive personalized feedback, regular support, and use reflection as a means for changing beliefs, behaviors, and practices in the classroom.

In other educational contexts, coaching has become increasingly popular in school districts as a way to change teaching practices and impact student learning. School districts employ literacy coaches, STEM coaches, math coaches, and general instructional coaches to help teachers grow and refine their teaching craft. In the coaching literature, coaches are described as "catalysts" that bring transformation in a system through fostering relationships, holding meaningful conversations, and using reflective feedback. As a GT coach, you, too, can be a catalyst for change by transforming potential into realized talent through partnered work with teachers.

Coaching in the Context of Gifted Education

Many gifted education programs use collaboration models such as "push-in," co-teaching, co-planning, etc. to incorporate intentional differentiation in the regular education classroom. In many districts the role of the gifted teacher is expanding to that of a differentiation (or enrichment) coach. We spend time unpacking the definition of a GT (Gifted/Talented) coach in Chapter 2, but to provide direction on where we are going, we introduce it here:

> GT coaches are change agents, specifically co-thinking partners who improve instructional practices by building capacity in other educators to identify, serve, and challenge high-potential students.

Consistent with Every Student Succeeds Act's (ESSA) criteria for professional learning, coaching can promote sustained, collaborative, goal-aligned, and transferable active learning for classroom teachers. Coaching also aligns with the National Association for Gifted Children (NAGC, 2019) standards and provides opportunities for regular follow-up and reflection (NAGC Professional Learning Standard 6.4.2). This can lead to more equitable approaches to identify, serve, and teach gifted and high-potential students, especially those from underrepresented groups.

It is important to note that coaching is a type of collaboration, but not all types of collaboration are forms of coaching. Collaboration hinges on the idea that both parties are "co-laboring" towards a purpose. In coaching, this co-laboring is in the form of co-thinking, and at times, this co-thinking leads to co-action (such as co-planning and co-teaching).

We emphasize this because sometimes teachers consider modeling, co-planning, and co-teaching synonymous with coaching, but coaching in the context of our book involves facilitating a teacher's growth from where they are to where they want to be through guided reflection. Sometimes co-teaching (two teachers planning and providing instruction) is not necessarily used to guide a teacher towards reflective growth; it is simply a collaborative practice using shared decision-making about student learning. Likewise, modeling and co-planning are excellent collaborative practices, but they are not always tied to the larger purpose of building capacity unless this is the intentional aim. To be clear, coaching can involve modeling, co-planning, and co-teaching, but coaching is overall a more encompassing approach to supporting a teacher's self-directed growth. Ultimately, the coaching process facilitates self-reflection to build capacity in *future* planning and teaching.

Coaching is also different from consulting. "Consultation is a collaborative effort between the gifted education teacher and another educator where the 'consultant' (i.e., gifted education teacher) provides direct guidance to the collaboration partner" (Mofield & Phelps, 2020, p. 10). As we discuss throughout this book, the role of a coach is not to give direct advice; rather, coaches support other teachers through guided reflection.

Collaborative practices also include team collaboration through inquiry groups such as Professional Learning Communities (PLCs) and other problem-solving teams (e.g., developing individual education plans). GT coaches can play a key role in the inquiry process of PLCs as teachers discuss next steps for student learning. PLCs or other forms of professional learning also provide opportunities for coaches to present strategies and other information about gifted/high-potential students and follow-up about their use and impact through the coaching process.

GT coaching starts with creating awareness. Figure 1.1 shows a continuum of coaching ranging from a focus on teacher-behaviors to deeper coaching with a focus on student outcomes. The focus moves from coaching how the teacher teaches to how students learn. To the left, sharing resources might be an entry point for collaborative coaching, but we emphasize that sharing a resource is not a true form of collaboration because it does not involve actual co-*laboring*. For example, if a coach simply emails a teacher a resource, this is not collaborative coaching. It can, however, serve to create awareness for teachers as a starting point in the coaching process, especially if the resource is used as a tool to ignite self-reflection.

Next along this spectrum is modeling. For a teacher to gain confidence in learning a new strategy, sometimes they benefit from seeing the strategy directly used with students. The modeling brings awareness to teachers by allowing them to see what the strategy looks like in action with students. It is represented on the side of more teacher-centered reflection because the emphasis is on building the teacher's awareness and skills.

The next level includes the co-action of co-planning and co-teaching as part of the coaching process. Because the conversations involve planning for student learning, the reflective process becomes more about how instructional decisions affect students, and so, this lands on the side of more student-centered reflections. Eventually, coaching can involve analyzing the impact of new practices on student learning through examining data, student work, and other student outcomes. Here, coaching conversations move from simply promoting awareness of instructional strategies to deeper explorations of supporting student growth.

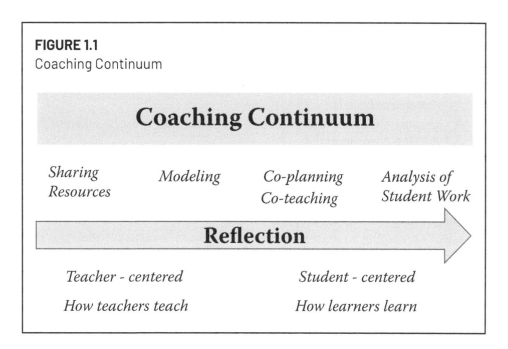

FIGURE 1.1
Coaching Continuum

Coaching Continuum

| Sharing Resources | Modeling | Co-planning Co-teaching | Analysis of Student Work |

Reflection

| Teacher - centered | Student - centered |
| How teachers teach | How learners learn |

Keep in mind that every teacher you work with will need various levels of support. For some teachers, you may start out sharing a resource in a PLC, or you may work one-on-one with a teacher who wants to co-plan with you to develop a tiered assignment for a group of clustered students. The continuum allows you to consider what the next step might be in supporting the teacher and to aim towards the deeper levels of coaching, focusing on using knowledge to make decisions that affect student outcomes.

Coaching through the Lens of Talent Development

We have previously described some realities in gifted education, specifically as they relate to students receiving differentiated instruction in regular education classrooms. GT coaching can indeed serve to empower classroom teachers to differentiate for gifted students. However, the possibilities of GT coaching move into broader contexts and issues in the field.

In much of this book, we focus our attention on using GT coaching in the context of the talent development model in gifted education (Subotnik et al., 2011). Specifically, this model emphasizes the following:

+ Giftedness is developmental and malleable.
+ Abilities matter and are both general and domain-specific.

+ Giftedness moves from potential to competence to expertise (or creative productivity in a domain).
+ Psychosocial skills (i.e., intellectual risk-taking, ability to manage stress, persistence, etc.) are levers to talent development and should be deliberately cultivated.
+ Opportunities and access matter. Opportunities must be taken to fully develop one's potential.
+ Early identification of potential in a given domain is important as this sets a student on a trajectory for continued growth (Subotnik et al., 2018).

Overall, the aim of talent development is to provide opportunities that cultivate a student's emerging strengths and talents. Because it takes on the view that giftedness is malleable, its goal is not about merely "meeting the needs" of the identified gifted students; rather, the goal is to provide contexts for giftedness to emerge, even if it is not currently seen. Advanced learning and enrichment experiences are provided as a means to nurture possibilities that might bloom into achievement.

Differentiation is still a necessary part of supporting advanced learning, but it is a *means* to cultivate talent, not an *end* of itself to provide specialized intervention to alleviate a need. Though this might appear to be a small nuance, talent development can promote more buy-in among teachers, administrators, and other school personnel in providing opportunities for students beyond those formally identified as gifted. Rather than focusing on ways to create specialized interventions for gifted students, this model casts a wider net so that more students might benefit from advanced learning opportunities. Thus, the talent development lens offers promise in promoting equitable access to advanced learning experiences.

> The talent development model acknowledges that typical characteristics of giftedness may manifest differently in high-potential and high-ability learners who are CLED, low-income, and/or in some categories of disability. It also acknowledges that abilities (general intellectual and in specific domains) are malleable and can be cultivated and nurtured by opportunity. Talent development, with its emphasis on developing potential early within domains, is one plausible option for not only enhancing opportunities to identify gifted students across all racial, ethnic, language, and economic groups as well as some categories of disability and to serve them appropriately, but also for achieving greater equity in gifted education in the United States and beyond.
> (National Association for Gifted Children, 2015, p. 12)

Through this framing, coaching in gifted education presents an opportunity for the field to address issues of equity, align goals with other district initiatives, and promote meaningful change in how we identify and serve high-potential students, especially those from underrepresented groups.

Coaching is Not in a Vacuum

If you are establishing a program within your district to incorporate a form of GT coaching, it is important to remember that coaching does not take place in a vacuum. Its purpose should be articulated and tied directly to facilitating progress towards the goals of the district and gifted program (see Chapter 7 for specific ways to align coaching to program goals). As classroom teachers engage in professional learning throughout the year, tied to a specific purpose and goal, coaching allows for the "follow-through" so that teachers take ownership and develop confidence in applying their new learning. Figure 1.2 shows the interaction between the district and school goals, the goals of the GT program, and coaching. The coaching process facilitates the movement for district and program goals to be

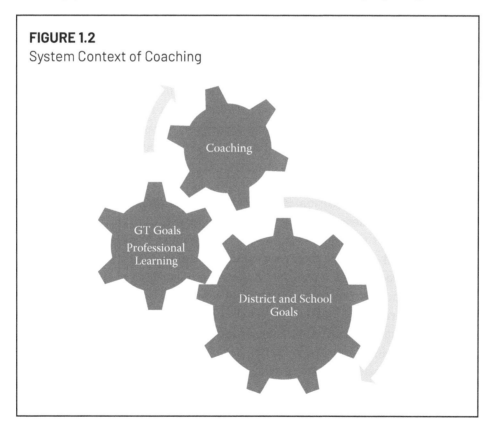

FIGURE 1.2
System Context of Coaching

attained. With coaching, the goals of a district become more than words on a page. The coaching ignites action that directly affects student learning.

As you will see in the coming chapters, GT coaching involves guiding a teacher to develop a goal for improving instruction. Yet, without knowledge about what to improve, it is unlikely the teacher will have the awareness to create a goal related to differentiation. For example, if a teacher has no knowledge of using pre-assessments for compacting, then it is unlikely that the teacher will be able to improve these practices. Coaching assumes that teachers interact with new knowledge before *and* while coaching takes place. Teachers may learn this new knowledge from a professional learning session, a resource shared by the gifted education teacher, PLC session, webinar, book study, or other professional learning activity. As leaders of a school, district, and gifted program align their goals with strategic plans for professional learning, the follow-up coaching can facilitate the transfer of knowledge to application. In this way coaching can be used to reinforce these practices with an individualized approach.

The Benefits of Coaching

Coaching is a dynamic, reflective process of leading change. Why is it so powerful? First, it is a form of individualized professional learning. It's really "differentiation" for adults! As we explain throughout the book, GT coaching revolves around teachers' own professional needs and goals. Unlike attending whole-school in-services in which teachers arrive from a variety of entry points, experiences, and contexts, coaching is a personalized learning experience.

Additionally, the principles of GT coaching are rooted in adult learning theory. Adult learning literature points to self-directed learning as an adult learning preference. This involves identifying learning needs, accomplishing set goals, and evaluating success (Gilson, 2018; Merriam et al., 2007). The GT Coaching Circuit (which we describe in Chapters 4–6) provides a number of opportunities for teachers to have ownership as they establish their own goals, select strategies, tweak them for their own contexts with students, and refine them. Coaching works because it transfers ownership of learning to the teacher. The teacher is empowered to apply, reflect, and refine practices that lead to lasting change in instructional practice. To coach means to help others find their own power and connect to their own sense of agency (Aguilar, 2013).

Classic research from Joyce et al. (1987) and Joyce and Showers (1995) showed that transferring new learning from professional development into actual practice increased to 80–90% when coaching was added to the use of theory, demonstration, and practice as part of the teacher's learning experience.

Additionally, teachers who receive coaching were shown to have students with higher gains in achievement compared to students with teachers who had not received coaching (Joyce & Showers, 1982). These results, however, are not necessarily seen immediately. Research has also shown that coaching effects are greater on student achievement when coaching is implemented over time (Marsh et al., 2008).

Coaching can also pave the way for building a climate of collective capacity within a school and district. This promotes a culture of collective commitments as more and more school personnel see their role is to support the learning of every child in the school. In this way, the benefits of coaching are tied not only to building capacity in a classroom teacher, but also in driving shared decision-making at the school and district level (we discuss more of this in Chapter 7).

The Change Process

We have presented some promising benefits of coaching, but as we know, not all teachers will eagerly participate in this process. Why might this be? When we discuss GT coaching, we are really talking about teachers *changing* practices. Change requires individuals to get out of their comfort zones and change their routines and behaviors. Behaviors are tied to beliefs, but changing beliefs for the long-term is indeed deep work. However, beliefs about student learning do not necessarily need to change at the onset of coaching. Changing teacher beliefs happens *throughout* the coaching process. For example, a teacher may change beliefs after reflecting on the direct effect of new instructional practices on student outcomes (Vargas & Melvin, 2021).

Understanding the process of change can help as you tackle your role as a GT coach and provide some context for why the models that follow are keys to managing the change. Remember that change is a "process," and changes in instructional practice do not happen overnight. In fact, some of the research in coaching shows that it might take up to three years to see the effects of coaching on student achievement (Killion et al., 2012).

There are many theories of change management. A key assumption is that for change to occur, a person must have the will, skill, knowledge, and the capacity to change. Fortunately, coaching can build all of these (Aguilar, 2013). It builds "will" (volition) through empowering teachers to make their own decisions. It builds skill and knowledge through modeling, feedback, and reflection, and it builds one's capacity to change by fostering contexts through relationships where teachers feel safe to take risks and change their practices.

GT coaching is part of a larger organizational aim for change (i.e., change in instructional practices to affect student learning). As we have previously described, GT coaching is one important gear interacting with other gears of a larger system. This interaction brings momentum in actualizing the vision and mission of the district goals and gifted services goals. Organization change, however, does not happen without individual change. The ADKAR Model (if you haven't noticed, we certainly like acronyms!) (Hiatt, 2006) is a change management model used to guide individuals through a change process. It notes that individuals must achieve five outcomes for change to occur. We have applied this model within the GT Coaching Circuit. Each part of the acronym is described here to relate to coaching practices:

+ Awareness: Teachers discern a need to "change practices" through self-reflection, facilitated using third point tools, self-assessments, student data, or follow-up from recent professional learning, etc. This is also an opportunity to identify beliefs connected to the thinking of the teacher. From the coaching experience, an awareness of current beliefs and practices emerge, and so, it creates a context for moving towards change.

+ Desire: Teachers decide to engage in the process of coaching because they see its value in how it affects their own professional growth and student outcomes.

+ Knowledge: Teachers grow in their knowledge of strategies and skills to support gifted/high-potential students because of the support offered in learning and applying new strategies.

+ Ability: Teachers develop confidence in their skills to differentiate (self-efficacy) as they receive ongoing support and engage in reflective practice.

+ Reinforcement: The change "sticks" because the coach partnership happens over time and the goals of the teacher are revisited. The coach and teacher celebrate the growth that occurs.

As you learn more about GT coaching in this book, keep in mind that the big picture of coaching is to bring about transformation in instructional practices, particularly in how gifted/high-potential students are identified and served in the regular education classroom. We intentionally situate the GT Coaching Circuit (Chapters 4–6) in the ADKAR model so that the change in teaching practices has a long-term impact on student learning.

TEAM Framework

The driving force behind coaching, and collaborative practice in general, is that relationships matter. Keep in mind that the spark of change often begins in conversation. As such, when building coaching relationships, it is important to work from a set of principles that guide the process of creating productive relationships. The TEAM framework (Mofield, 2020; Mofield & Phelps, 2020) provides the context to engage in these conversations (see Table 1.1). From the onset of establishing early coaching partnerships, these principles provide the space to build a safe, respectful, and proactive collaborative relationship.

TABLE 1.1
TEAM Framework for Collaborative Practice

T	Trust
E	Engage Each Other's Expertise
A	Align Beliefs and Values
M	Maintain the Relationship

Trust

Trust is transformative. In the same way that a teacher strives to create a positive learning environment for students to take risks in their learning, GT coaches also need to remain mindful of the importance of establishing trust within coaching conversations. Remember that many teachers may not have a strong background in understanding the needs of gifted and high-potential learners, so it is possible that some might feel overwhelmed or not prepared to initially engage in these conversations.

What are some key considerations to begin to develop these trusting relationships with colleagues who might be hesitant to begin the coaching process? The first step is to recognize that there is not one magic word or secret handshake that will open the door to meaningful and impactful coaching. There are, however, several key ideas. Think of these guiding factors as a "Trust

TABLE 1.2

Trust Toolbox: Guiding Considerations

Guiding Consideration	Putting it into Practice
Give trust to receive trust.	+ Strive to be transparent. This provides an opportunity to have shared "power" within coaching conversations. + Enter conversations with the mindset that you are working alongside knowledgeable, capable, and well-intentioned professionals. + Allow yourself to be vulnerable and seen as one who is continuing to grow and learn.
Lead with respect.	+ Respect the profession, your colleagues, and the process. + Remain mindful that sometimes people are dealing with issues that we know nothing about.
Acknowledge progress.	+ Help others recognize personal growth and impact on student learning. + Celebrate the growth of the collaborative partnership.
Don't overpromise.	+ Be clear on what is possible, probable, and realistic. + Create certainty through clear expectations vs. generalities of what might be considered the best-case scenario.
Lead with humility.	+ Begin conversations with positive energy through statements such as *I'm thankful we have this time to meet*, or ask how they are doing. + Let your collaborative partners know that you will honor their time.
Show appreciation.	+ Let your collaborative partner know that you appreciate the opportunity to work and grow together. + Share with your collaborative partner how you have learned from your joint, collaborative work.
Be authentic.	+ Be true to who you are and what your core values are while also respecting your collaborative partners' ideas, insights, and values.

Toolbox" of sorts that help you reflect on your own practice while also considering the culture, dynamics, and values of your district, building, and individual colleagues (see Table 1.2).

By working from these guiding considerations, trust develops deeper levels of reflection within the coaching process. This brings alignment between the collaborative partners and organizational values (Ray, 2017; see Figure 1.2).

Engage

Remember that coaching is a partnership where GT coaches and teachers are equals, recognizing that every teacher brings a level of expertise to the coaching conversation (Knight, 2019). It is through this process of *engaging* each other's expertise that all collaborative partners have an opportunity to grow and evolve. A teacher's expertise might be focused on grade level standards, knowledge about the curriculum, knowledge of students, or specialized content. Likewise, the expertise of a GT coach might be founded in gifted pedagogy, differentiation strategies, characteristics of gifted learners, expertise on twice-exceptional learners, or the NAGC Gifted Programming Standards (2019). As you engage through coaching conversations, prioritize the following principles:

+ Engage each other in the planning process.
+ Value each other's expertise.
+ Ask questions.
+ Listen to ideas.
+ Build from one another's ideas.
+ Offer encouragement and praise.
+ Engage to actively address unspoken assumptions of each individual.

It is through this engagement of expertise and co-thinking that new ideas emerge, allowing for the *aha* moments of reflection.

Align

In many ways, coaching conversations are like a stream of teacher-driven, reflective productivity, and like any "stream," there are barriers that might figuratively stop the flow of co-thinking during this process. For this reason, it is important to align beliefs with your coaching partners from the onset of the coaching process. Take the time to align beliefs regarding such things as student discipline, teaching styles, and expectations for all involved. Also, discuss each other's values (e.g., obtaining high achievement scores, accelerating content, aligning lessons to students' interests) and communication styles.

Aligning does not equate to agreeing on everything, but it does mean that all involved are working toward an "and" rather than an "or" approach to the collaborative work.

Throughout this process of aligning beliefs, assumptions should also be a key consideration, as assumptions impact how coaching relationships evolve. At a basic level, assumptions are based on an individual's belief system and life experiences. These assumptions often guide an individual's instructional decision-making. For example, some educators hold the assumption that all gifted students will be perfectly fine with current instructional practices within a regular education setting. Those who hold this assumption would be more hesitant to seek out additional support through coaching. Likewise, some may hold assumptions that students with disabilities cannot also be gifted (i.e., twice-exceptional learners). Again, it is important to have these conversations and align beliefs as much as possible prior to engaging in the coaching process. As Covey (2015) outlines, "seek first to understand" while aligning and addressing any underlying belief systems and assumptions of collaborative partners.

Maintain

"Maintain" in the TEAM framework includes integrating regular opportunities to engage in reflective discussions focused on what is working well, as well as exploring how to improve areas that need extra attention. Throughout these conversations, be open to feedback and seek to provide descriptive rather than evaluative feedback. While there are times that these "maintaining" conversations might be difficult, keep in mind that coaching partners are further empowered by hearing varying perspectives and investing in the time to address issues (Ray, 2017). In addition, one of the most powerful components of maintaining the coaching relationship is to help each other recognize and celebrate the positive steps and successes throughout the coaching process.

Establishing a Vision

As you reflect on the foundations of GT coaching as outlined in this chapter, take a moment to envision these practices within your own context. Perhaps you have already served in a coaching role for several years and are excited about continued growth, or perhaps you are brand new to the field of coaching.

You might be starting in a new district, hold a new position, or work alongside colleagues with whom you have known for years. What is your experience and background in meeting the needs of gifted and high-potential learners? What are the backgrounds and needs of your collaborative partners, as well as the students you serve? How do these factors impact the vision you have for yourself as a GT coach?

As you proactively create this vision, think about what you hope to achieve as a GT coach. Perhaps you might have heard of, or even made, a vision board. A vision board provides an opportunity to take what you "wish" for yourself and create a visual representation of how you can make it a reality. Vision boards:

+ Provide clarity.
+ Empower follow-through.
+ Remind us of our goals.
+ Keep us focused.

Whether you choose to actually create a true vision board to keep at your workspace as a visual reminder or choose to journal and/or reflect on your future vision as a GT coach, consider the following:

+ What are your beliefs about how students learn?
+ What are your beliefs about how adults learn?
+ What does "building capacity" in others mean to you?
+ How do you empower yourself to continue to grow, learn, and evolve within the field of gifted education?
+ How do your values impact your goals, communication, and instructional decisions?
+ What visual images or metaphorical representations illustrate the goals you have for yourself as a GT coach?

These are just a sample of reflective questions to consider while creating your future goals, insights, thoughts, and visualization of responses to set the stage for next steps.

As you connect your own personal vision to the foundations of GT coaching outlined in this chapter, a greater clarity of how you can better identify, teach, and support gifted and high-potential students will emerge. In addition, as you begin to apply these coaching principles to your own context, the subsequent chapters of this book will provide clear structures and next steps to support you in this transformative role. Before continuing with your reading, take the time to reflect upon the following questions as you relate GT coaching to your own personal experience.

Reflection Questions

1. Have you ever received coaching? What has been your own experience with coaching in the past? What components of the TEAM framework were or were not present?
2. In your context/school, to what extent does differentiation happen in the regular education classroom? What barriers exist for teachers at your school?
3. In what ways does your GT program adopt talent development practices? Why might the framing matter in establishing a GT coaching program?
4. What is the relationship of coaching to the school, district, and GT program's goals in your district?

References

Aguilar, E. (2013). How coaching can impact teachers, principals, and students. Edutopia. https://www.edutopia.org/blog/coaching-impact-teachers-principals-students-elena-aguilar.

Aguilar, E. (2020). *Coaching for equity: Conversations that change practice.* Jossey-Bass.

Callahan, C.M., Moon, T.R., & Oh, S. (2014). National surveys of gifted programs: Executive summary 2014. National Research Center on the Gifted and Talented.

Covey, S. (2015). *The 7 habits of highly effective people.* Free Press. (Original work published 1989.)

Gilson, C. M. (2018). Moving toward differentiated professional learning for teachers learning to differentiate for gifted students. In A.M. Novak, & C.L. Weber (Eds.) *Best practices in professional learning and teacher preparation: Vol. 1. Methods and strategies for gifted professional development* (pp. 93–120). Prufrock Press.

Hiatt, J.M. (2006). *ADKAR: A model for change in business, government and our community.* Prosci Research.

Joyce, B., & Showers, B. (1982). The coaching of teaching. *Educational Leadership, 40*(1), 4–10.

Joyce, B., & Showers, B. (1995). *Student achievement through staff development: Fundamentals of school renewal.* Longman.

Joyce, B., Showers, B., & Rolheiser-Bennett, C. (1987). Staff development and student learning: A synthesis of research on models of teaching. *Educational Leadership, 45*(2), 11–23.

Killion, J., Harrison, C., Bryan, D., & Clifton, H. (2012). *Coaching matters.* Learning Forward.

Knight, J. (2007). *Instructional coaching: A partnership approach to improving instruction.* Thousand Oaks, CA: Corwin.

Knight, J. (2019). Instructional coaching for implementing visible learning: A model for translating research into practice. *Educational Sciences, 9*(2), 101. https://doi.org/10.3390/educsci9020101.

Marsh, J., McCombs, J., Lockwood, J.R., Martorell, F., Gershwin, D., Naftel, S., Le, V., et al. (2008). *Supporting literacy across the sunshine state: A study of Florida's middle school reading coaches.* RAND Corp.

Merriam, S.B., Caffarella, R.S., & Baumgartner, L.M. (2007). *Learning in adulthood: A comprehensive guide* (3rd ed.). Wiley.

Mofield, E. L. (2020). Benefits and barriers to collaboration and co-teaching: Examining perspectives of gifted education teachers and general education teachers. *Gifted Child Today, 43*(1), 20–33. https://doi.org/10.1177/1076217519880588.

Mofield, E., & Phelps, V. (2020). *Collaboration, coteaching, and coaching in gifted education: Sharing strategies to support gifted learners.* Prufrock Press.

National Association for Gifted Children. (2015). *National Association for Gifted Children talent development task force: Report to the board of directors.* http://www.nagc.org/sites/default/files/Governance/TalentDevelopment TFReport_11%2003%2015_FINAL.pdf.

National Association for Gifted Children. (2019). *Pre-K–Grade 12 gifted programming standards.* http://www.nagc.org/sites/default/files/standards/ Intro% 202019%20Programming%20Standards.pdf.

National Association for Gifted Children. (2019). *2019 Pre-K–Grade 12 gifted programming standards.* http://www.nagc.org/sites/default/files/standards/ Intro%202019%20Programming%20Standards.pdf.

Ray, B. (2017). Educational leadership coaching as professional development. *School Leadership Review, 12*(1), 29–38. https://scholarworks.sfasu.edu/slr/ vol12/iss1/5.

Subotnik, R. F., Olszewski-Kubilius, P., & Worrell, F. C. (2011). Rethinking giftedness and gifted education: A proposed direction forward based on psychological science. *Psychological Science in the Public Interest, 12*, 3–54.

Subotnik, R.F., Olszewski-Kubilius, P., & Worrell, F.C. (2018). The talent development framework: Overview of components and implications for policy and practice. In P. Olszewski-Kubilius, R.F. Subotnik, and F. Worrell (Eds.),

Talent development as a framework for gifted education (pp. 7–23). Prufrock Press.

Vargas, L., & Melvin, R. (2021). Four myths on coaching and efficacy. *Educational Leadership, 79*(3). https://www.ascd.org/el/articles/four-myths-on-coaching-and-efficacy.

Chapter 2

What is a GT Coach?

Perhaps you are reading this book because you have found yourself in a new role as a GT coach. You have tremendous potential to advocate for gifted learners and expand your influence on student learning. You may be wondering, what does it mean to be a GT coach? In this chapter, we define this role. Beyond describing the actions of a GT coach, we also describe the guiding beliefs of a coach (i.e., the coach's mindset), a lens for thinking about relationships with others, and how core values shape beliefs and actions. These beliefs, thoughts, and values are applied to the actions within the GT Coaching Circuit, a flexible structure for coaching other teachers through a reflective process.

Coaching in gifted education can indeed lead to transformation, but this happens only if the soil is ready. Structures, supports, and conditions must be right for a GT coach to be effective. Part of the structure involves establishing the role of a GT coach. To emphasize the need for a clear definition of this role, we share (with permission) the content of an email we recently received from a teacher (to protect anonymity, we call her Carla) who has transitioned into a new role of a coach in gifted education. As you read it, consider the various obstacles she faces.

> I am a gifted resource teacher . . . In my position, I have recently transitioned from a GT Teacher role to a coaching/teaching role. I wear several hats. I split my time between teaching

DOI: 10.4324/9781003340560-3

pull-out and coaching. Unfortunately, I have never been trained on how to do the latter, so I have been figuring it out as I go.

I am learning that teachers and administrators are not concerned about the educational performance of my gifted learners. I am just at a loss! The word 'differentiation' gets thrown out at every PLC, yet differentiation is not happening, and I don't know how to help! I have held sessions to teach them differentiation strategies, shared the difference between gifted myth and reality, and I have presented information on the identification process for our county. I provide differentiation tips via email and provide semester newsletters. I also offer to meet with them to discuss strategies. Unfortunately, it seems as though they all want a "quick-fix." They want something that I can hand them, and I can't keep up. I cannot make a choice board/menu for each subject and grade. I have one grade-level that seems to take me up on my offer, but sadly, that is it. Each grade-level extends their "thank yous" but rarely does anything change . . .

The statement "rarely does anything change" is the hardest statement to read. We all want to feel like we are making an impact on students and that our actions lead to success. When we don't feel like we are making an impact, it's easy to throw in the towel and give up.

There are several parts of this email that many gifted education teachers can relate to: she has several roles, she is eager to share new information, but others do not take her seriously, and she is extremely knowledgeable about serving gifted students. She also expresses a concern that is shared by many instructional coaches- she is figuring out what it means to be a coach along the way. We will revisit many of these obstacles throughout the book, but first, we address clarifying the role.

So, I'm a GT Coach. What does this mean?

To answer this question, first, let's discuss coaching broadly in education. Coaching has become increasingly popular in schools as a way to support teachers in implementing new initiatives, developing new skills, and improving instructional practices. Some schools employ cognitive coaches, whose primary aim is to support teachers to become aware of how they make decisions in their instructional practices through self-reflection, self-evaluation, and self-directed learning. Transformational coaching, associated with the work of Elena Aguilar, is also well-known in school districts and focuses on supporting a teacher in understanding how beliefs, behaviors, and "ways of being" influence instruction.

Most of our work is based on infusing gifted education with instructional coaching. Based on the work of Jim Knight, instructional coaching involves two teachers (one in the role of a coach) acting as partners to improve learning and teaching in the classroom. Instructional coaching uses a dialogical approach to facilitating coaching conversations. This means that the coach guides the teacher through reflective feedback and questioning but also provides direction as needed. We believe this approach is a good fit with gifted education given that many classroom teachers do not have training related to gifted education pedagogy. As we will describe later, other more facilitative coaching models rely on leveraging a teacher's knowledge and skills to guide reflection on teaching. In the context of GT coaching, however, what good is it to have teachers reflect on their use of differentiated teaching practices if there is not a base of knowledge of best practices to work from? Therefore, we apply instructional coaching to GT coaching and offer our formal definition here:

> GT coaches are change agents and co-thinking partners who improve instructional practices by building capacity in other educators to identify, serve, and challenge high-potential students.

Let's consider a few key words from this definition. To be clear, GT is referred to as "Gifted and Talented" as this is often used in titles to refer to gifted education teachers and specialists. GT coaches are referred to as change agents in our definition. They are catalysts for changing practices through reflective feedback and guided questions. GT coaches are facilitating change for equitable identification, expanding opportunities for more students to be provided high-quality robust instruction, and purposefully planning for differentiated instruction in response to students' needs.

The etymology behind the word "coach" means "to carry." This brings to mind old-fashioned carriages that transport people to their destination. Likewise, a GT coach serves as a vehicle to carry a teacher from their current state of reality to an aspirational state. The destination, or goal, is determined by the teacher, not the coach. The coach is there to "smooth the way" for the teacher, serving as a guide to facilitate thinking, action, and self-reflection along the journey (Costa & Garmston, 2015).

Notice, the definition characterizes GT coaches as co-thinking partners. This means they think *with* the teacher and serve beside them (not above them) with shared power, shared decision making, and shared understanding. The GT coach has no higher status in relation to the teacher. The partnership emphasizes the shoulder-to-shoulder approach in working towards the teacher's goal.

The definition also emphasizes building capacity. You will see this phrase continually throughout this book. Coaching is effective because it goes beyond "sharing resources" with teachers. Coaching brings lasting change by empowering teachers to use and create these resources effectively in the future.

The last part of this definition leverages the expertise that a GT coach has about best practices in gifted education. Though the list that follows is not exhaustive, the role of a GT coach might include supporting teachers in the following areas:

+ Talent-spotting by identifying gifted behaviors and student strengths.
+ Co-planning high-level rigorous lessons.
+ Co-planning differentiated assignments.
+ Selecting or adapting curriculum for advanced learners.
+ Co-developing enrichment learning activities.
+ Sharing best practices on acceleration.
+ Designing assessments.
+ Using data to reflect on students' next steps in learning.
+ Providing reflective feedback.
+ Modeling mini lessons.
+ Developing tiered assignments.
+ Making instructional decisions.
+ Setting up mentorships for students.
+ Addressing affective/social-emotional needs of students.
+ Developing interventions for underachievement.

One goal of a GT coach is to maximize access to high-level learning opportunities in regular education classrooms. This has the potential to benefit not only identified gifted students in these classrooms, but also students who are not formally identified as gifted. For example, the GT coach may work with the classroom teacher to embed more elements of critical thinking into questions and learning activities. This benefits all students. As a result, more students have opportunities to practice critical thinking and show how they are making insightful connections within the content. The impact of coaching is long-lasting as the teacher is now equipped with a model for teaching critical thinking to not only current students but also future students in years to come.

Additionally, the GT coach may work with the teacher on making decisions to select and adapt the content to which critical thinking and creative thinking are applied. This is coaching for differentiation where readiness levels are considered to ensure all learners have an opportunity to be challenged at the "just right" level. This might include selecting more advanced resources, higher level texts, or more open-ended tasks for students to grapple with more complexity in their learning.

We emphasize that the role of the GT coach is not limited to supporting the teacher in differentiating only for individual students who are identified as gifted. We view the GT coach's role as situated in the talent development model as described in Chapter 1. Through this talent development lens of coaching, a teacher at your school might shift from seeing you as the gifted specialist who works only with gifted students to someone who is knowledgeable about practices that help all students grow and thrive. By maximizing access to high-level learning in regular education classrooms, conditions are ripe for talent to emerge. Through the talent development lens, the GT coach supports the teacher in providing high-quality, rigorous instruction so that all students have opportunities to show their budding strengths and talents across content areas.

Coaching Mindset

The beliefs of a coach drive successful coaching. Based on coaching literature (Costa & Garmston, 2015; Kee et al., 2010; Killion et al., 2012; Knight, 2018), effective coaches 1) recognize their own need for continued growth and learning and 2) believe in the unlimited potential of others to grow and learn. When these beliefs are acted upon, we see coaches who can be described as empowering, humble, encouraging, positive, trusting, confident, reflective, and inspiring. If a coach truly believes in the unlimited potential of others, then they are operating on the assumption that people don't need to be "fixed." Fixing people is the opposite of what effective coaches do. When coaches offer advice rather than work through the reflective process of coaching, it undermines the confidence and self-worth of others.

When serving as a GT coach, the goal is not to "give advice." Instead, the goal is to give the teacher a mirror to reflect on their own teaching practices. Thus, the coach must have exceptional communication skills to ask the right questions, guiding the teacher to process through *aha* moments, realizations, and next steps. Throughout this book, we will revisit this metaphor of a mirror as it is essential for creating ownership of new practices. This is quite different from giving a teacher "advice" or always "showing a teacher what to do." Advice is toxic! It might be important to write this in bold on a sticky note, posted in a place as a daily reminder. Giving advice does not allow the teacher to grapple with figuring out what to do and robs the teacher of an opportunity to have agency of their own behavior. Also consider, what happens when teachers follow your advice, and it doesn't work? Perhaps they may not trust you in future collaboration.

We must be reminded that the language we use constructs reality. If we frame our interactions with teachers as "providing help" to teachers, then we may be unintentionally establishing a context for building dependency rather than capacity in the teacher. The goal is not to "fix" a teacher, but to support a teacher in their own learning and growth. The coach should not be doing work *for* the teacher; the coach is providing a mirror for the teacher to think about next steps towards reaching a self-selected goal.

On a related note, just as it is important to use asset-based language when supporting students, we can likewise use asset-based language when describing how to support teachers. The language we use when we speak (and even think) reflects our beliefs regarding what other teachers can do and what they are capable of. Table 2.1 shows a contrast between deficit and asset-based language applied to coaching teachers.

TABLE 2.1
Deficit vs. Asset-Based Language

Deficit Language	Asset-Based Language
The teacher can't	The teacher can
I can't be expected to	How can I better communicate?
I tell the teacher___, but he/she doesn't____.	I can better engage ___ by___.
There is no way . . .	It might be possible to . . .
The teacher does not ____.	The teacher's strengths are____

SCARF: Understanding Threats to Coaching Relationships

We have established that GT coaches see the unlimited potential in teachers. Even with the most positive mindset, coaching will have its challenges because it involves human beings working with other human beings. Both sides of coaching (receiving and providing) involve vulnerability, trust, and risk-taking. Reflective practice is difficult to achieve if the teacher feels threatened in the collaborative work. Fortunately, when we understand the invisible dynamics underlying these challenges, we can work to alleviate them.

SCARF is an acronym created by David Rock (2008) to describe factors that affect human behavior in social situations. Specifically, these are threats and enhancers to relationships.

Using this lens for coaching will illuminate how to navigate challenging situations and proactively create contexts to leverage them as enhancers. As defined by Rock, SCARF stands for:

+ S – Status: Your relative importance to others.
+ C – Certainty: Your ability to predict the future.
+ A – Autonomy: Your sense of control over events.
+ R – Relatedness: How safe you feel with others.
+ F – Fairness: How fair you perceive the exchanges between people to be.

If we think back to the email in the introduction of this chapter, we can see a number of instances in which these elements are at play. First, Carla's role is not taken seriously by those she's working with. It is clear that Carla's status is threatened because she does not feel valued by her colleagues. Carla explains that she is in the new role of a coach and is "figuring it out" as she goes. There is obviously a lack of certainty as she is not able to clearly establish her role as a GT coach. Teachers are likely uncertain of what to expect of her in this new role.

Carla explains that in this new role her time is split between being a coach and a pull-out teacher. We wonder if Carla had any choice in any of the new changes. She states she has had no training, which implies that she has had no choice (from the district level) on how to learn and grow as a new coach. When Carla describes that other teachers simply want "quick-fixes" this conveys a tone that the teachers only value what she can do for them. There is little evidence of a strong, positive relationship between her and the teachers. Finally, we see the threat of fairness in her sharing that she does so much work in sharing and presenting strategies to teachers, but this work is not perceived to be appreciated. Who would not be frustrated in this situation? As we zoom out and consider the overall context, we can see that conditions, supports, and structures must be in place to enable successful coaching.

In order for GT coaching to be successful, it is important to consider contexts so the answer is a "Yes" for both the coach and the teacher for each question:

+ S – Status: Am I valued?
+ C – Certainty: Can I depend on___?
+ A – Autonomy: Do I have a choice?
+ R – Relatedness: Do you care?
+ F –Fairness: Am I respected?

In the chapters that follow, the structures, communication skills, and models are developed to enhance the components of SCARF. Even in the definition of GT coaching, *status* is considered with the phrasing "co-thinking" partner, emphasizing that the coach's role is not one with more power than the teacher. Establishing the role of the coach and outlining the GT Coaching Circuit (in the sections that follow) establish *certainty*. This model includes a number of ways to increase teacher *autonomy* in the coaching process, creating opportunities for teachers to share their input and choice as to how they instruct students. Further, the communication skills in Chapter 3 enhance *relatedness* and *fairness* as they are rooted around the ideas presented in the TEAM framework (Trust, Engage, Align, Maintain).

Self-Awareness: Understanding Core Values

While SCARF provides a lens for thinking about interpersonal relationships with others, it is also important to have strong intrapersonal self-awareness of your own driving core values. As a GT coach, you may encounter many challenges, but through understanding the core values that drive your behaviors and actions, you can stay centered on the motivations behind your decisions.

We encourage you to take a moment to look up "core values list" through a simple internet search. Consider the words that stand out and resonate with you. Which ones especially lead you to do what you do? If you can, narrow the list down to three to five core values. As you reflect on what motivates you, how do these core values come into play in your life (both professionally and personally)? How do these core values show up in your behavior? In your interactions with others? In what ways are you triggered when you do not get to act through your core values?

Here, Emily reflects on a recent experience where a core value took a hit:

> Recently as I was preparing to teach a graduate class in person, many students emailed me an hour before class started to explain that they would be attending class "remotely" through Zoom since it was raining outside. This certainly triggered frustration for me as I had to figure out how to balance more than half the class in person and half the class online. After working through my own frantic frustration, I reflected on why this triggered such an emotional response. Because I value excellence, having to prepare to teach half my students online and half in person at the same time at the last minute was a threat to the excellence I strive for in my teaching. I felt I could not bring "excellent" instruction in this context, and so my immediate response was to be frustrated with my students.

When we understand our own values, we understand what's truly important to us and also what triggers us. This type of self-awareness also brings insight into our interactions with others. On the surface, it might appear that coaching is about teaching another teacher how to use strategies in their classroom; however, deeper levels of coaching involve bringing to the surface beliefs behind behaviors. When we are attuned to paying attention to the core beliefs and values of those we are coaching, we can understand the link between their values and actions. Values are evident in how individuals make decisions, so a coach might consider "What do their actions reveal about what they believe?"

For example, when encountering resistance or a complaint, you can identify a value behind that complaint. If a teacher is resistant to incorporating more critical thinking into instruction because critical thinking is not assessed on the state standardized assessment, then the coach might identify that the teacher values student accomplishment, especially through the performance on the test. The coaching conversation can involve affirming that the teacher indeed values student success. If the coach can pinpoint what the teacher values, then this value can show up in co-thinking with the teacher other ways to define and measure student success (Gross Cheliotes et al., 2018). This is discussed further in Chapter 3 regarding reframing resistance.

A key to building buy-in to adopting new teaching practices (such as more rigorous instruction matched to student readiness levels) involves understanding what other teachers value and leveraging these values to achieve the overall aim of providing robust instruction for all students, including gifted/high-potential students). Thinking about teachers through a coaching mindset involves approaching coaching conversations with an understanding that teachers are highly committed to student success! Through affirming what you hear they are committed to (e.g., student relationships, equity, achievement), you can better support teachers in reflective growth.

Dialogic Coaching

Earlier, we mentioned there are different types of coaching. On one end of the spectrum is facilitative coaching which assumes the teacher already has the knowledge of instructional practices to implement. The coach facilitates the teacher's thinking by supporting them to become aware of what they already know (Whitmore, 2002). In cognitive coaching practices, the facilitative coach guides the teacher to uncover mental maps for decision-making and facilitates reflection on developing self-developed solutions.

On the other end of the spectrum is directive coaching where the coach's role is to share expert knowledge with the teacher so the teacher can master a specific skill. In essence, teachers are told what to do and how to do it. Knight notes, "directive coaching tends to de-professionalize teaching by minimizing teacher expertise and autonomy, and therefore, frequently engenders resistance" (Knight, 2018, p. 12).

Dialogic coaching, however, is a balance between the two. We believe facilitative coaching would not work well in the context of GT coaching because many teachers do not already have the knowledge about differentiating for advanced learners in the classroom. They indeed need some direction in implementing differentiation strategies and would not be able to uncover this through deep self-reflection. Yet, based on the TEAM framework (i.e., engage expertise) and what we understand about interpersonal relationships (i.e., SCARF), a complete directive approach is not conducive to supporting status, autonomy, or relatedness.

In dialogic coaching the coaching happens through "dialogue." The coach does not purposefully withhold expertise from the teacher. Instead, the coach provides best practices and research in gifted education but positions the teacher as a decision maker (Knight, 2018). If the coach only provides advice on what to do, this would not be a dialogue. On the other hand, if the coach withholds expert knowledge that would help guide the teacher towards better serving gifted/

TABLE 2.2

Levels of Coaching: Activating Possibilities

Level	Coach's Action	Activating	Prompts
Red Light	+ Giving Advice	+ You should___.	+ Here is how you__. + Do this, not that.
Yellow Light	+ Teaching/ Sharing Ideas	+ How might we__? + You might__. + We could___.	+ Would you like to explore some options together? + You could consider a, b, or c. What criteria needs to be considered?
Green Light	+ Listening, Questioning, Reflection	+ How might you__?	+ You are saying____. You seem to value____. + What are your next steps? + What if __?

Adapted from Kee et al. (2010).

high-potential students, this would not be dialogue either. Therefore, when considering the definition we have of GT coaching, we emphasize the "co-thinking" partnership that is critical to this dialogical collaborative approach.

In Table 2.2 we show the Green, Yellow, and Red light levels of coaching. The Green light level (bottom) demonstrates a more facilitative approach. Much of a coaching conversation may cruise through the Green light level as the coach listens and asks reflective questions. However, there are times when teachers need guidance and direction. In the Yellow light level (middle), the coach can slow down and move coaching into a teaching space. Perhaps the teacher needs to learn more about effective teaching practices for gifted/high-potential learners. This might be an opportunity for a teacher to see a strategy modeled, or the coach may give the teacher direct feedback on an aspect of instructional design. Best practices should be shared, but notice that even in the Yellow light, autonomy is honored by first asking if the teacher is willing to explore a number of ideas. In the Yellow light, the goal is to co-construct knowledge with the teacher, not simply share and tell information. This is still quite different from the Red light level of advice giving. This approach is too directive and might only apply if the teacher is outright disrupting student learning.

The GT Coaching Circuit

The GT Coaching Circuit Overview is shown on p. 38 (Resource 2.1) (see Appendix A for the full GT Coaching Circuit and coaching notes for each stage). This provides a big picture view of what a coaching circuit includes in the context of supporting a teacher's skills to identify, support, and challenge gifted/high-potential students.

GT Coaching Circuit Overview

Set a Purpose	Plan and Act	Reflect
Establish a student-focused goal	**Select and learn a strategy**	**Reflect on student learning and next steps**
Evaluate Need –Determine Need: *As you think about the gifted/high-potential students in your classroom* + What do you know about their readiness levels? Strengths? + *What do they need to progress in their learning? How do you know?* + What are their next steps in learning? + *On a scale from 1–10, how well do you think ____? Why did you not say 1? What would it take to increase your confidence?* + When you think about challenging every student in the classroom, what gets in the way? **Establish Goal** + Goal- *What are you wanting students to do and understand?* + Criteria- *What might this look like?* + Baseline- *Where are students already in relation to this goal?* **Explore Ideas** –Create a Focus Question + *In what ways might ____? How might students ____?* –Brainstorm + What ideas do you have already? + Would you like to brainstorm ideas together?	**Select a Strategy** –Choose a strategy to implement, considering its purpose and impact on student outcomes. + *How does the desired student outcome align with the purpose of the strategy?* + *How does the strategy engage gifted and high-potential students as a means to increase academic achievement and student growth?* + *How does the strategy provide opportunities for students to make connections, problem-solve, or accelerate their learning?* – Use the Tool Template: *What, Why, How* – Elicit teacher input with GT Instructional Blueprint: + *How do you think you might modify this with your students?* **Support the Teacher in Learning the Strategy** –Discuss options for co-action: + Model the strategy (bite-sized modeling). + Co-teach the strategy through a shared vision. + Co-plan a lesson with the teacher. **Set up for Success** –When the teacher is ready, the teacher uses the strategy in own planning and instruction. –Provide reflective feedback on use of strategy (if requested).	**Reflect on Goal Attainment** –Revisit the Goal + *What was the goal? To what extent did students achieve it?* –Reflect on Evidence + *How did the selected strategy impact gifted and high-potential students? Other students? Reveal talent and recognize student strengths?* + *In what ways did you observe students showing creative thinking? Critical thinking? Making connections?, etc.* **Reflect on Building Capacity** –Make connections between student outcomes and teacher decisions + *When you did ____, what did you notice from students?* **Reflect Forward** –Celebrate –Transfer to new contexts + *How might this strategy be used in other content areas? with a different group of students?in an upcoming unit?* –Revise Goal/Plan Next Steps + *What are your next steps?* + *Do you want to revise the goal?* + *When can we meet again?*

This model is based on some of our previous work on collaborative practices in general. As part of our work in 2020, we introduced the Collaborative Process Model as a framework for guiding various kinds of collaboration including co-teaching, co-planning, coaching, and collaboration with parents and other community members. As shown in Figure 2.1, this model includes three steps in a sequence: set a purpose, plan and act, and reflect, based on a shared understanding of how each individual contributes to the collaboration, and situated within the TEAM framework. The entire GT Coaching Circuit follows this sequence, based on the shared understanding of the role of the coach and the role of the teacher (to share their ideas, lesson plans, and content expertise). As mentioned in Chapter 1, it also follows the ADKAR model for change – building an awareness and desire for change, strengthening knowledge and abilities, and reinforcing skills for long-term learning and transfer.

Notice that we use the word "circuit" rather than cycle. While our approach does indeed show a cycle where the process is continually repeated, the idea of a circuit implies other nuanced meanings. By definition, a circuit (Circuit, n.d.) is "a circular journey or one beginning or ending at the same place." As a GT coach

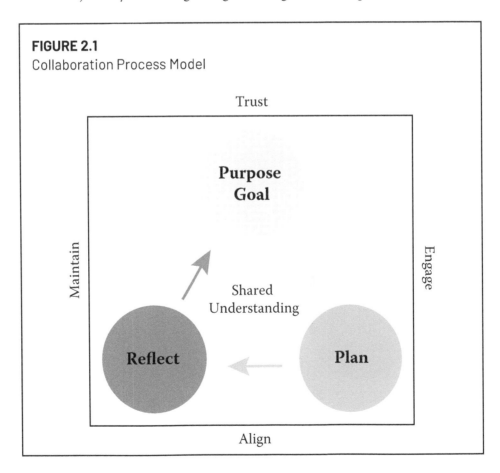

FIGURE 2.1
Collaboration Process Model

guides a teacher through set a purpose, plan and act, and finally, reflect, the partners come together to revisit the goal, ending the circuit where they started. Its definition also implies a roundabout course and journey. This is especially appropriate in our description because we are cautious of indicating this process as a set sequence of steps. As you guide a teacher through this process, it is imperative to approach all coaching encounters with flexibility in a way that responds to the needs of the teacher.

We also might think of electric circuits, which are paths for transmitting power or electrical currents. In the context of coaching, the coaching conversations that take place at each stage (i.e., Set a Purpose, Plan and Act, Reflect) open pathways for new information to transmit and provide "power" to the teacher's capacity. The coaching circuit is a way to connect a teacher to new knowledge by way of interaction and constructing new knowledge with the coach.

The word circuit is also associated with "circuit training" in sports. Circuit training is a workout technique that involves a series of exercises for strength-training and muscular endurance. In coaching, this metaphor explains how coaching conversations focus on developing and strengthening skills of a teacher to support high-potential students. Each part of each stage is like an exercise (e.g., Set a Purpose – Evaluate Need, Establish Goal, Explore Ideas) that builds know-how in applying differentiation strategies.

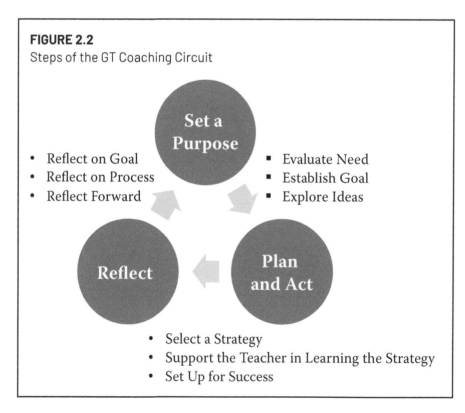

FIGURE 2.2
Steps of the GT Coaching Circuit

Chapters 4, 5, and 6 outline these "exercises" or stages within the GT Coaching Circuit. We present a visual of each of these steps within each stage of the circuit in Figure 2.2. Though it is not intended to be used as a prescriptive guide or checklist, we do intend for it to be used as a flexible structure to focus your work on coaching for change in gifted education. As you read the pages that follow, it is important to keep in mind that coaching is individualized professional learning; this means that the time it takes to move through each stage of the circuit can vary widely from teacher to teacher. Some parts of the circuit may only take 7–10 minutes (e.g., establish a goal, explore ideas) while other parts of the circuit could take much longer (e.g., co-planning). As a GT coach, it is important to be responsive to the teacher's progression of learning. We provide a scenario in Appendix B to show an example of how a GT coach and a teacher might engage in dialogue through each stage of the coaching circuit.

First Steps to Lasting Change

The first steps in the coaching circuit set the stage for creating lasting change. By taking the time to identify and address these first steps, coaching conversations will be more authentic and targeted to the needs of the teacher and their students. In addition, these first steps serve to create a greater sense of certainty (i.e., SCARF) to the process, while also providing opportunities to leverage a teacher's strengths and build collective efficacy in meeting the needs of gifted/high potential learners.

Many of you might be familiar with the popular Waze app that is often used as a driving navigation system. As with many navigation apps, Waze alerts you of an obstruction on the roadway, identifies where heavy traffic is, or even signifies if there is a live animal on the side of the road while also providing alternate pathways to help you arrive at your destination with the least amount of resistance, stress, and worry. Just imagine if there was a similar app for GT coaching, one where you would know exactly who to seek out, what strategies would be needed, and even where to locate gifted students who have yet to be identified. While there is clearly no app to help in this process, GT coaching extends beyond what any app could provide by building capacity to address the needs of gifted/high-potential learners across time, contexts, and applications of practice. The following sections provide an overview of key considerations in this process. Note that many of these ideas are expanded upon throughout subsequent chapters. We share them here as a birds-eye view of the "map" for the upcoming journey.

Team with Administrative Support

Gaining support from administration is key in promoting successful GT coaching and collaborative practice. This support creates and promotes a culture that recognizes and celebrates student achievement, commitment to learning, and an inclusive learning environment (Donohoo et al., 2018). As you seek to gain and develop this ongoing support, work to address the following:

+ Develop an appropriate master schedule that allows for coaching/collaboration on a regular basis. In doing so, collaborative practice becomes a recognized and valued practice within the building.

+ Plan for cluster grouping to support student learning and minimize the number of classes to navigate scheduling concerns.

+ Provide and support professional learning opportunities and encourage active participation. These opportunities need to embrace long-term goals vs. "in the moment" thinking (Hargreaves & Fullan, 2012).

+ Raise awareness of the benefits of GT coaching. As administration begins to be an advocate for GT coaching, there is a greater opportunity for talent development for all learners.

More specific suggestions for creating collaborative shared plans and establishing the GT coaching vision for the school can be found in Chapter 7.

Create Clear Expectations

Certainty continues to be a foundational step leading to strong GT coaching practices. As you begin to engage in new coaching conversations, work with your collaborative partners to develop norms. Norms might include items such as starting and stopping on time, using respectful dialogue, and avoiding distractions during coaching sessions. In addition to developing norms, it is also imperative to talk about what coaching is and what coaching is not. It is possible that there might be erroneous assumptions about coaching that need to be clarified. In addition, engage in dialogue with your collaborating teacher to clarify roles and designate responsibilities of the GT coach and teacher. These might consist of tangible responsibilities that need to be completed between coaching sessions, as well as responsibilities focused on confidentiality, respect, and commitment.

Work with the Welcoming

When starting out, find those who are open and willing to engage with GT coaching. Teachers can often be reluctant to engage in a collaborative process such as coaching when they have been "volun-told" to do so by administration (Mofield & Phelps, 2020). There are also those who might not just be ready yet to engage in the process. Be patient, and over time, those participating in GT coaching will begin sharing their positive experiences, and others will want to join in to reap the same levels of personal and professional growth. More about addressing resistance is discussed in Chapter 3.

Be Flexible

GT coaching is not a one-size-fits-all approach. Be prepared to expect the unexpected. Remember, coaching is focused on a teacher's self-selected goal, not what the GT coach already has in mind. Listen to what each teacher shares about their objectives, their students, and the areas that they value. Work with each teacher to recognize the needs of their gifted/high potential students. It might be that a class needs more opportunities to engage in critical thinking or have additional experiences to examine diverse perspectives across interdisciplinary units of study. Perhaps students would benefit from curriculum compacting or working through tiered learning activities. Regardless of the needs, the teacher should always feel empowered and autonomous in selecting their student-focused goal, and at no time should they feel as though they are being led down a predetermined path (Ray, 2017). Remain steadfast in the understanding that GT coaching is "an individualized process, uniquely co-constructed by each coach and teacher" (Knight, 2019, p. 7). In doing so, teachers will feel more valued and empowered.

Engage in Strength-Based Collaboration

Success in coaching stems from leveraging the shared expertise and strengths of both the GT coach and the teacher. Remember that coaching relies on co-thinking, co-planning, and co-action in working toward a teacher-selected goal. As coaching conversations focus on addressing the needs of gifted and high-potential learners, remember to ask yourself, "How is the teacher able to contribute their knowledge of advanced content, current assessment data, knowledge of students, and structures and expectations within their classroom to the coaching conversation?" Likewise, how will you, as a GT coach, be able to leverage your knowledge of strategies, NAGC Programming Standards, and gifted pedagogy to support the teacher in their student-focused goal? It is through a shared understanding that coaching conversations synthesize expertise through reflective practice and meaningful dialogue. This is what builds capacity and leads to positive student outcomes.

Respect Autonomy

Classroom teachers often find comfort in having a sense of control over their classrooms. In many ways, classrooms reflect what teachers value in education and hope to pass-on to their students. Imagine if someone just came into your home and decided to redecorate with their own ideas and preferences. If that happened, you would probably kick them out and lock the doors. A similar reaction might occur if coaching leads with telling teachers what to teach, how to teach, and how to best engage students in the learning process. All these actions would threaten a teacher's sense of autonomy and potentially impact their self-worth and sense of identity. In turn, there would be a greater potential for conflict. As such, when you engage in coaching conversations, lead with respect, and ensure that teachers have a say in how they differentiate, which strategies would work best with their students, and how to best accelerate their students, amongst other things. GT coaching is not meant to manipulate teachers into meeting the needs of gifted/high-potential learners, it is a means to empower teachers as change agents. GT coaching is a catalyst to create agency in teachers to recognize their options as they grow in awareness of talent development for all students.

Reflection Questions

1. Reflect on Carla's email. In what ways do you have a similar experience? What threats are at play in your own experience? How might you work to address these threats?
2. What systems of support are in place to prepare you for successful coaching? What additional supports are needed? What is in your control, out of your control, and within your sphere of influence? What next step might you take within your control?
3. What are the implications of other classroom teachers viewing you in a role beyond a specialist working only with gifted students to that of a GT coach (in supporting talent development)?
4. Reflect on your core values. What happens when your actions and your core values are not aligned? How do these core values come into play in your collaboration with others? How can recognizing others' values enhance your coaching practices?

References

Costa, A. L, & Garmston, R. J. (2015). *Cognitive coaching: Developing self-directed leaders and learners* (3rd ed.). Rowman & Littlefield.

Circuit (n.d.). Dictionary.com. https://www.dictionary.com/browse/circuit.

Donohoo, J., Hattie, J., & Eells, R. (2018, March 1). The power of collective efficacy. ASCD. https://www.ascd.org/el/articles/the-power-of-collective-efficacy.

Gross Cheliotes, L.M. & Reilly, M.F. (2018). *Coaching conversations: Transforming your school one conversation at a time* (2nd ed.). Corwin Press.

Hargreaves, A., & Fullan, M. (2012). *Professional capital: Transforming teaching in every school.* Teachers' College Press.

Kee, K., Anderson, K., Dearing, V., Harris, E., & Shuster, F. (2010). *Results coaching: The new essentials for school leaders.* Corwin.

Killion, J., Harrison, C., Bryan, D., & Clifton, H. (2012). *Coaching matters.* Learning Forward.

Knight, J. (2018). *The impact cycle: What instructional coaches should do to foster powerful improvements in teaching.* Corwin.

Knight, J. (2019). Instructional coaching for implementing visible learning: A model for translating research into practice. *Educational Sciences*, *9*(101), 1–16. https://doi.org/10.3390/educsci9020101.

Mofield, E., & Phelps, V. (2020). *Collaboration, coteaching, and coaching in gifted education: Sharing strategies to support gifted learners.* Prufrock Press.

Ray, B. (2017). Educational leadership coaching as professional development. *School Leadership Review*, *12*(1), 29–38. https://scholarworks.sfasu.edu/slr/vol12/iss1/5.

Rock, D. (2008). SCARF: A brain-based model for collaborating with and influencing others. *NeuroLeadership Journal*, *1*, 78–87.

Whitmore, J. (2002). *Coaching for performance. GROWing people, performance, and purpose.* Brealey.

Chapter 3

Coaching Conversations

This chapter describes the important communication skills used in coaching. Whether you serve as a gifted education teacher and/or a GT coach, the use of these skills builds trust, strengthens relationships, and leverages the elements of SCARF (see Chapter 2) to enhance the coaching relationship. While we provide a model for an entire coaching circuit, we want to emphasize that coaching does not necessarily follow this linear sequence. Coaching happens in conversations and even through email, texting, and PLC meetings. Every moment of communication is an opportunity to build a teacher's awareness and capacity to grow.

Committed and Active Listening

Coaching conversations require a foundation of trust. As discussed in Chapter 1, TEAM provides the framework to build trust, as well as a means to engage, align, and maintain a healthy collaborative relationship. Each attribute of the TEAM framework is reliant on committed listening. In essence, committed listening prepares a path to understand what the collaborative partner is sharing, valuing, and feeling. It identifies the "real" message behind the shared words.

DOI: 10.4324/9781003340560-4

Listening is an integral factor in successful GT coaching. In the field of education, the phrase "active listening" is often referred to as the type of listening we need to engage in, but the nuances between active and committed listening actually elicit very different responses. First and foremost, coaching conversations are a dialogue, or stream of meaning, between collaborative partners working from a shared vision. This is in stark contrast to a discussion, which shares the same root as "percussion" or "concussion," meaning to break things up (Bohm & Rickles, 2014).

Discussion requires active listening, but the intent and commitment to listening is quite different. Discussion creates the need to be listening with the intent to respond with evidence to back up a personal point of view or position. Dialogue, however, leads with committed listening where there is a shift from listening to *respond* to listening to *understand* (Gross Cheliotes & Reilly, 2018).

Committed listening stems from the *intentionality* of listening. It is important to listen with a full awareness that listens not only for spoken words, but also for the emotions and values that are at the root behind the words. It is not uncommon for those new to the GT coaching role to have to retrain how they engage in listening in order to empower teachers through productive coaching conversations. This level of intentionality creates a space for collaborative partners to feel heard, valued, and appreciated. Committed listening keeps the teacher's shared insights, experiences, and thoughts at the center of the coaching conversation. This, in turn, provides a great deal of insight and information as to how to engage the teacher in their next steps.

Counterproductive Listening

Counterproductive listening involves behaviors and inner dialogue that take the listener away from the objective of being fully present, purposeful, and committed within the GT coaching role. Within the context of this book, we specifically focus on autobiographical, judgmental, inquisitive, solution-focused, and counterproductive listening (Costa & Garmston, 2015; Kee et al., 2010).

Autobiographical Listening

GT coaching involves creating collaborative relationships, and as a result, autobiographical listening is a counterproductive behavior that is an easy trap to fall into. Autobiographical listening stems from the need to relate to others. While this active type of listening often begins with the intent to hear what the collaborating teacher is sharing, the commitment to listening is lost as the GT coach begins to think of and interjects a personal story as a way to connect. Perhaps the teacher is feeling overwhelmed with navigating the needs of twice-exceptional learners, or the teacher might be reaching out to problem solve how to manage stations to appropriately integrate more tiered learning activities, but through autobiographical listening, the focus is taken away from exploring those needs. Unfortunately, when the GT coach begins to focus on their own personal experience, the coaching session turns from a teacher-centered focus to a coach-centered focus. In turn, the GT coach loses an opportunity to support the teacher in developing capacity to grow.

Judgmental Listening

Through this form of counterproductive listening, the GT coach "tunes-in" to the perceived flaws or perceived lack of awareness of the collaborating teacher. This creates an inner dialogue for the GT coach that takes precedence over what the teacher is sharing. Not only does this divert committed listening away from the teacher, but it also channels deficit thinking in the GT coach. In addition, it has the potential to lead to authoritarian overtones, creating long-lasting, negative effects on the collaborative relationship. Within gifted education, judgmental listening often stems from a place of frustration, feeling that others may not have the awareness or understanding of the needs of gifted learners. For example, if a teacher is sharing excitement about having gifted learners peer-tutor other students in the class, this is not a time to feel frustrated that the teacher is not meeting the needs of gifted students. Instead, through committed listening, celebrate that the teacher is sharing an *awareness* of gifted learners in the class and *values* that a different approach is needed. This opens up a purposeful dialogue regarding the needs of gifted learners and bridges the conversation into *how* gifted/high-potential learners can be provided with new and challenging learning opportunities to engage with advanced content.

Inquisitive Listening

Inquisitive listening happens when the GT coach begins to focus more on the "why" a situation is occurring rather than purposefully listening to the content of what the teacher is sharing. Because this creates a separate inner dialogue in the GT coach, the resulting conversations often do not align with the teacher's original need. Take, for example, a teacher who is asking how to use pre-assessment data to determine flexible grouping for an upcoming lesson. A GT coach engaging through inquisitive listening might ask the teacher a series of questions: Why is flexible grouping important? Why should gifted students be provided with autonomous learning activities? How might you create a menu of options for differentiated enrichment? None of these are negative conversations to engage in, but the GT coach missed the mark on fully listening to the teacher's original question about how to use pre-assessment data to inform flexible grouping. The teacher was not heard, and a co-thinking opportunity was lost.

Solution-Focused Listening

Without question, GT coaches seek to build teacher capacity to better meet the needs of gifted and high-potential learners. Remember, however, that it is detrimental for GT coaches to work from an advice-giving stance. Within this form of counterproductive listening, the GT coach intently focuses on how to solve a problem, instead of committing to listening to what the teacher is sharing. While the intention is meant to be positive, solution-focused listening undermines a teacher's opportunity to reflect and grow within their own instructional practice. As with the previous scenario of a teacher asking how to use pre-assessment data to determine flexible grouping for tiered learning tasks, a GT coach engaging in this counterproductive listening might launch directly into different options for alternative learning activities, such as independent research, thinking as a disciplinarian through a real-world problem, or creating an interdisciplinary problem-based learning scenario. Again, these are all valid options for curriculum compacting, but the immediate need of the teacher was not addressed.

Listening with Commitment

Understanding the common forms of *counterproductive listening* can prepare you to remain aware of the *committed listening* needed for proactive GT coaching. Take a moment to reflect on past conversations and collaborations that you have had. Are you able to relate to one or more of the aforementioned counterproductive listening behaviors as either the speaker or the listener? Table 3.1 provides examples of how these different forms of counterproductive listening might impact the GT coaching process. As you engage with the GT Coaching Circuit in Chapters 4–6, we encourage you to consider your own listening behaviors and how those behaviors might impact the dynamic flow of the circuit. Much of the time, these behaviors stem from wanting to relate to and "help" others.

TABLE 3.1

Counterproductive Listening Examples

Counterproductive Listening Type	Teacher's Shared Thoughts	Counterproductive Tendencies & Implications	Committed Listening Focus
Autobiographical Listening	"I have a twice-exceptional student in my class who has not been completing work. I don't know what else to do. I just need to let the SPED teacher deal with the situation."	Inner-dialogue and the resulting coaching conversation focus on the GT coach's personal, related experiences. This sabotages the teacher's opportunity for self-reflection and discovery. "I hear you. I had a student last year who had ADHD and this is what I did."	+ What are the emotions behind the shared thoughts? + What are the underlying values behind the shared thoughts? + How might the teacher's shared thoughts lead to teacher reflection toward a student-focused goal? + What aspects of the teacher's shared thoughts provide a lens for further teacher reflection?
Judgmental Listening	"When my gifted students complete their class-assigned math problems, I have packets of similar problems to keep them busy vs. being a distraction to others."	Inner-dialogue and the resulting coaching conversation focus on the GT coach's feelings of frustration and deficit thinking, inhibiting the coach to guide self-discovery. This results in condescending coaching conversations. To self-"I can't believe she is giving packets! Rigor is not more work, but *different* work!"	
Inquisitive Listening	"After seeing you model a Socratic seminar with advanced content, I tried it, but my students just didn't participate. I don't know if I planned it correctly."	Inner-dialogue and the resulting coaching conversation focus on the GT coach's use of excessive questioning that depart from the core of the teacher's shared thought. "Mrs. Smith uses the fishbowl method in Socratic seminars. Have you seen her use it? Do you get to visit other teachers' classrooms?"	
Solution-Focused Listening	"I have a very diverse class this year, and I was thinking that learning stations might be a way to differentiate, but I have no idea where to begin."	Inner-dialogue and the resulting coaching conversation focus on the GT coach's ideas of how to address the issue. The GT coach acts as the decision maker rather than the teacher. The teacher loses the opportunity for self-reflection. "You should try the RAFT strategy! My students loved it last year!"	

Coaching in Gifted Education

Presuming Positive Intent

Presuming positive intent has a profound impact on a person's perception of status (i.e., SCARF; see Chapter 2). At its most basic level, presuming positive intent focuses every conversation through understanding that each collaborative partner is capable, knowledgeable, and well-intentioned. Take a moment to reflect on those words: capable, knowledgeable, *and* well-intentioned. Presuming positive intent views all of those attributes as a whole, not just one or two. This can often be a challenge depending on past interactions with a teacher, the culture of the building, or even one's own personal values and philosophies. To help put this into context, you might be able to relate to a time when someone did not perform well on a particular task, and another individual commented in a somewhat condescending manner, "Well, at least they meant well." While this might not seem overtly negative, the statement holds an underlying tone that the individual might not have been capable or knowledgeable in the first place. This mindset has the propensity to create a threat against a person's status and can greatly impact future collaboration. Through presuming positive intent, you remain mindful that you are working with capable, knowledgeable, and well-intentioned teachers seeking to improve their instructional practice.

To communicate through presuming positive intent consider that the syntax of questioning impacts an individual's status and the degree to which

TABLE 3.2
Presuming Positive Intent

Instead of	Consider
+ Have you. . .? + Could you. . .? + Do you. . .? + Can you. . .?	+ What. . .? + Which. . .? + As someone who. . .? + When. . .? + In what ways. . .? + Given. . .?
Example: Have you thought about why your gifted and high-potential students are not completing their assigned work?	Example: Given what you know about your gifted students' interests and readiness levels, how might that information be used to plan for engaging learning experiences?

Adapted from Kee et al. (2010).

capacity can be further developed. For example, asking yes/no questions can sometimes be perceived as demeaning, while asking open-ended questions can be perceived as inviting. Table 3.2 provides example sentence stems that reflect presuming positive intent in contrast to questions that could elicit feelings of threat or defensive attitudes.

Presuming positive intent creates the opportunity to engage in dialogue focused on building capacity with the collaborating teacher. For example, a teacher might share a frustration stemming from gifted/high-potential students not completing their work. If the GT coach responded with "Have you thought about why they are not completing their work?" the teacher's response might be defensive and along the lines of, "Of course I have! Why do you think I'm here?" In contrast, if the GT coach engages the teacher by asking, "Given what you know about your gifted students' interests and readiness levels, how might that information be used to plan for engaging learning experiences?" the resulting coaching conversation could lead into co-thinking and co-planning towards a solution.

The Power of Paraphrasing

As discussed earlier in this chapter, committed listening plays a key role in successful GT coaching. While committed listening informs questions that build capacity and guide coaching conversations with teachers, a GT coach cannot *only* rely on strong questioning. If the coach only asks questions, this can make the teacher feel as if they are being interviewed or are experiencing an "inquisition." Coaches must also develop the skill of paraphrasing.

A coach serves as a "mirror" for a teacher to reflect on instructional practice. Paraphrasing is a key skill to facilitate this mirroring. The term means "to tell back" and can be used as a way to re-voice what the teacher shares in a conversation. While paraphrasing does not mean to parrot back word for word what a teacher communicates to you, it does show that you have listened intently to what the teacher is sharing, particularly to the ideas, values, and assumptions.

Thoughtful paraphrasing reflects the ideas and emotions behind the words. For example, Cheliotes and Reilly (2018) explain that when teachers complain, they are often committed to the opposite of what they are complaining about. If a teacher shares that they do not have time to do all that is being asked of them, they really value a high standard of excellence, or if they vent that students are being tested too much, they are expressing a concern for student learning. A paraphrased statement such as "You are committed to a high standard of excellence for your students" can be especially affirming. This is yet another way that relatedness (i.e., SCARF) can be developed and nurtured within the coaching relationship, which in turn builds stronger trust as part of the TEAM framework.

Not only does paraphrasing build upon a solid foundation of trust, it is also a method of re-voicing what is being shared by the collaborating teacher to provide greater clarity and understanding of next steps. Through this re-voicing, the GT coach is sending the message: *I am listening. I am interested. I care. I am trying to understand your experience.* Through paraphrasing, the GT coach and collaborating teacher are better prepared to launch into next steps because the focus has become clearer. This clarity, in turn, contributes to a greater sense of certainty (i.e., SCARF).

Ultimately, coaching supports a teacher's thinking in instructional decision-making. GT coaches act as a conduit to clarify the teacher's thought processes. As a teacher voices inner thoughts into language, paraphrasing those thoughts back to the teacher brings a greater awareness to the teacher's own thinking processes. The paraphrasing, then, is itself a metacognitive tool to guide the teacher through self-awareness of how and why decisions are made.

To guide teachers to self-reflect on their own thinking, the following types of paraphrases can be used (Costa & Garmston, 2015: Kee et al., 2010):

+ Clarifying and Acknowledging: This type of paraphrasing is used to affirm values and emotions (as described previously) or to mirror back specific details to make sure you are on the same page with the teacher. When voicing back the underlying emotions or values, a teacher can feel affirmed and have an awareness of underlying motivations or thoughts behind their thoughts, decisions, and actions.

+ Summarizing and Organizing: After a teacher shares a great deal of information, a coach paraphrases the major themes and categories. As the content is organized, the teacher gains self-awareness of the more abstract matters at hand.

+ Conceptual Shift: Coaches use this type of paraphrasing to bring the conversation focus to a higher, more abstract level or to a lower, more concrete level. To bring to the abstract level, the coach states the major concepts, goals, and assumptions behind what the teacher shared (e.g., "You desire to teach students in their zone of proximal development"). If a teacher is discussing more generalities, the coach can paraphrase to name the specifics behind major concepts (e.g., "Differentiation is modifying the content, process, product, or environment").

Table 3.3 provides examples of how these types of paraphrasing are applied to coaching within gifted education contexts. Regardless of the type of paraphrasing that is used, the goal is to focus beyond the actual words that are being

TABLE 3.3

Types of Paraphrasing Applied to Coaching in Gifted Education Contexts

Clarifying and Acknowledging	Summarizing and Organizing	ConceptualShift
Identify the emotion conveyed and the content shared: + You're feeling. . . + You're thinking. . . + You're wondering . . .	Guide the teacher to understand how their thoughts are organized: + One one hand. . .on the other hand. . . + You are working through multiple steps . . .	Identify beliefs, values, assumptions, and perspectives to guide the teacher to new ideas or to clarify thinking: You seem to value. . . A major goal you have set for yourself is. . . You are concerned overall with . . .

Shared Comment	Paraphrase
My students come from such diverse backgrounds and have such varying readiness levels, I am struggling with trying to engage them all to meet their different learning needs. How can I manage meeting the needs of my gifted learners while I have students who are not even meeting grade level standards?	*You're feeling overwhelmed with the variety of learners' needs in your classroom.* -Clarifying and Acknowledging
Some of my most advanced students do not seem to be demonstrating all they are capable of. It's like they just don't seem to care anymore. What am I supposed to do?	*You're wondering how you can motivate and engage your students in their zone of proximal development.* -Clarifying and Acknowledging
Some of my students are beginning to recognize that there are different levels of work in my class, and I don't know how to handle that. I want all of my students to feel "smart." How do I make sure that differentiation does not make those who might be struggling feel inferior?	*On one hand, you recognize the value of differentiated instruction, but you are concerned with how to manage tiered learning in a manner that leverages each student's strengths.* -Summarizing and Organizing
I am still new to teaching and am having a difficult time juggling everything. I'm trying to assess my students' needs, plan for instruction, and demonstrate student academic growth. I feel like there are so many demands, and I don't even know where to start. I mean, how can I show student growth when some of my gifted learners are already in the 99th percentile?	*You are concerned overall with planning to meet the needs of all your students while also creating opportunities for gifted and high-potential learners to engage in advanced content to demonstrate academic growth.* -Conceptual Shift
I feel like I am constantly having to attend meetings, fill in for teachers who are out sick, and complete paperwork. When am I going to be able to plan to make sure that all of my students have access to a quality education?	*You seem to value a high level of excellence, and you are afraid you can't attend to all of your responsibilities in a way that meets the expectations you have for yourself as an educator.* -Conceptual Shift

Source: Adapted from Kee et al. (2010).

spoken to truly listen to understand what is being shared (Kee et al., 2010). When this happens in dialogue, it creates a space to co-construct meaning, especially as teachers interact with their own thoughts mirrored through the paraphrasing.

Reflective Feedback Through Ask-Affirm-Activate

Reflective feedback is the process of asking clarifying questions, valuing potential, and asking reflective questions (Perkins, 2003). Unlike evaluative feedback or constructive feedback, its intent is to guide a teacher to self-reflect about their own practices and next steps. Here we introduce a structure for reflective feedback based on Perkins's (2003) model. We call it Ask-Affirm-Activate:

+ **Ask questions for focus:** Ask questions to bring focus to the coaching conversation. These questions ensure that the GT coach and teacher are working from a shared understanding.
+ **Affirm potential:** Acknowledge positive elements of current practice while leveraging a strength-based approach to the possibilities that exist.
+ **Activate possibilities:** Uncover alternatives, explore different perspectives, and discover self-directed options.

We provide examples of prompts and questions in Table 3.4. Using this structure allows the coach to stay out of "advice mode" and focus on allowing the teacher to make meaning of their own experience. This is true "reflective" feedback, empowering the teacher to have realizations and *aha*'s about new ideas and alternatives. The Ask-Affirm-Activate structure can be used at any time during the GT Coaching Circuit. Since coaching can happen in a variety of contexts, it can also be a useful go-to model for short conversations in the hallway, PLC meetings, and even email communication.

While the structure of Ask-Affirm-Activate can be used at any point in the GT Coaching Circuit and can be somewhat fluid, it is important to remain mindful not to jump directly to the "activate potential" phase. As educators, activating potential is highly valued; however, without first asking questions for focus and affirming potential, the resulting collaboration might not provide the needed focus or validation that is needed to move forward in the most productive manner.

TABLE 3.4
Ask-Affirm-Activate

	Ask for Focus	Affirm Potential	Activate Possibilities
Coaching Prompts	+ What do you want to focus on? + In what ways might we?	+ You value____. + It's exciting to see____. + It's really important for you to___.	+ In what ways might___? + What..? How. . .? + What would happen if__? + What does that look like?
Example	*What is the content area you are wanting to focus on?*	*You value student ownership in their learning.*	*How will this create an opportunity for students to "think as an expert" in science?*

Source: Adapted from Perkins (2003).

Levels of Coaching: Activating Possibilities

Previously in Chapter 2, we described the Green, Yellow, and Red light levels of coaching (see Table 3.5). We have emphasized that the GT Coaching Circuit is situated in dialogical coaching. This means that there are times when the coach's role is not entirely facilitative of a teacher's own knowledge and capacities (Green light) but also not too directive in providing "help" and advice (Red light). In GT coaching, the dialogue between the coach and teacher may lead to opportunities for the coach to offer clarity or share resources, ideas, and input for the teacher to make informed instructional decisions. This falls under the teaching level (Yellow light).

The use of paraphrasing and providing reflective feedback through Ask-Affirm-Activate can be applied at each of these different levels, depending on the teacher's own knowledge and understanding of teaching gifted/high-potential students. For example, through paraphrasing in the Green light level, the re-voicing supports the teacher's ability to reflect on their instructional practice by further clarifying, organizing, or recognizing a conceptual shift in practice. This provides a heightened sense of validation and affirmation as a foundation for activating new possibilities in next steps. The question stems such as, "How might. . ." and "How will this impact. . ." can ignite new ideas for action. Though we have listed "What if" as a question to ignite possibilities, we caution that sometimes it's an underhanded way of giving advice (e.g., "What if you used depth of knowledge to plan your tiers?"). If "What if . . ." is used, be sure that it allows a teacher to consider the *implications* of shared ideas (e.g., "What if you use this strategy in your classroom; how will it need to be modified?")

Sometimes there is a need to build capacity for new learning within Ask-Affirm-Activate. Paraphrasing through the Yellow light level is a "teaching" level of coaching, allowing for more guidance as needed. This level provides an opportunity to first acknowledge and summarize what the teacher is sharing and then follow up with a reflective question to activate co-constructed new knowledge. This question would be focused on developing a deeper understanding of gifted pedagogy (e.g., gifted characteristics, skills, strategies) so the teacher is equipped with knowledge to make informed instructional decisions. For example, you may say, "It sounds like you are wanting to offer opportunities for your students to use creative thinking. Would you like to explore some ideas together? . . . How might we co-plan to incorporate some of these ideas? . . . We could . . ." By contrast, the Red light level should only be incorporated if the teacher's instructional practice is negatively disrupting student learning, as it is highly directive and does not allow for the level of reflection that is at the core of GT coaching.

TABLE 3.5

Levels of Coaching: Activating Possibilities

Level	Coach's Action	Activating	Prompts
Red Light	+ Giving advice	+ You should___.	+ Here is how you__. + Do this, not that.
Yellow Light	+ Teaching/ Sharing Ideas	+ How might we__? + You might___. + We could___.	+ Would you like to explore some options together? + You could consider a, b, or c. What criteria needs to be considered?
Green Light	+ Listening, Questioning, Reflection	+ How might you__?	+ You are saying____. You seem to value____. + What are your next steps? + What if __?

Source: Adapted from Kee et al. (2010).

Keys in Skillful Interpersonal Communication

We have highlighted a number of important communication skills in coaching: committed listening, presuming positive intent, paraphrasing, and reflective feedback through Ask-Affirm-Activate. A skillful coach will also use other verbal and non-verbal responses in coaching conversations:

1) Silence is a powerful tool for thinking. While it is easy to respond to a teacher after waiting only one or two seconds, waiting longer will allow for more creative, thoughtful responses. This restraint of impulsivity also communicates that you value and respect their reflective thought process. The extra few seconds can allow for more opportunities for the teacher to make important connections and realizations.

2) Paralanguage (vocal qualities, gestures, non-verbal behaviors) conveys meaning and attention in the conversation. Repeating a teacher's gesture can be a visual aid for reflection. Intentionally using "mirroring" can convey interest and congruence. This can be through matching posture, gestures, pitch, volume, rate, and inflection (Costa & Garmston, 2015).

3) Invite opportunity for extended reflection through prompts such as, "Tell me more" or "I'm curious about that . . ." These invitations allow the teacher an opportunity to process more of their own experiences in verbal expression of thought. You will see that in Chapters 4–6 we include resources for coaching notes that include coaching prompts. These phrases can be used when the next step is to activate additional thinking and reflection from the teacher or when you are not quite sure what to say.

Communicating with Those Who Resist Coaching

Despite your best efforts, not everyone is going to want to participate in a coaching partnership. The reality is that classroom teachers are overwhelmed with numerous responsibilities, or they may even be jaded from previous experiences with new initiatives or even coaching relationships. Depending on the culture of the school, some teachers may be hesitant to partner with you because they don't want to be perceived as a teacher who "needs help." Even though coaching is intended as a way to support continued growth, not necessarily to give "help," reaching out on any level involves vulnerability. Further, some teachers may believe that they are challenging their students at a sufficient level and so they don't need to do anything differently. Other teachers may simply be overwhelmed by all the responsibilities on their plates, or they simply do not perceive that partnering with you will be worth the time and effort. They may just want you to go away and let them be.

When considering why the teacher is resisting, we must think about why we ourselves have resisted anything in our own lives (whether it is an initiative in your work setting or even a personal change). Toll writes:

> When we ourselves resist, we believe it is because we are good people who care about our work, communities, homes, and institutions. But when others resist, we often believe they are lazy, unconcerned, uninformed, or difficult. In other words, resistance is good in the eyes of the resister, bad in the eyes of those being resisted.
>
> (Toll, 2008, pp. 119–120)

It is important to think about teachers who resist with a lens from the coaching mindset (mentioned in Chapter 2) – believing in the unlimited potential of others to grow and learn. Those who are resisting have a rationalized reason for doing so. GT coaches must be careful to approach resistant teachers with genuine presumption of positive intent. Teachers who resist really may have the best intentions for students, but they are not recognizing a *need* for partnering with you. They may think that their instruction is already adequately meeting the needs of all students, or they may resist out of fear because they do not want to expose how much support they really need. Understanding why they are resisting is the first step, and this requires a disposition of curiosity rather than judgment. This curiosity founded on presumed positive intent opens the door for breaking down resistance to engage the teacher

Resistance happens because there is a force at play; there is a conflict of sorts between the teacher and the force. Ask yourself, "What are teachers actually resisting? Is there something I am doing to promote this resistance?" Consider how the following actions or dispositions might unintentionally instigate resistance for some teachers:

+ An over-enthusiastic coach who presents GT coaching as a way to "help" the teacher "be better." This could convey the message that the teacher needs to be "fixed." Offering to help does not recognize the teacher's strengths to leverage.
+ A GT coach who creates tiered assignments or choice boards, etc. *for* the teacher (rather than *with* the teacher). This might create resistance

because the teacher will never have "ownership" in the collaborative process and is only the recipient of unsolicited help. The teacher may have the impression there is a "right way" to create tiered assignments and that the GT coach is the only one with expertise on how to do this. This leads the teacher to perceive there's really no value in a coaching relationship.

+ A GT coach who comes across as "preachy" by sharing the latest research in gifted education. This can cause resistance because teachers might perceive they've done things wrong, or they see the strategies as "one more thing" they have to use.

Responding to Resistant Teachers

Though teachers may explain they are too busy, they don't need your support, or they have already had training to work with gifted students, you can always keep the door open. At the very least, you might establish a relationship with them and ask if you can learn more about what they do in their classroom. For example, you might respond with, "Learning more about how you teach your content area is helpful for me so I can share what you are doing with other teachers. What are students doing in your classroom that makes you feel excited?" This can be an opportunity to listen for how you might leverage their expertise (i.e., TEAM) in future communication.

Using many of the communication tips discussed in this chapter, you can sow seeds of trust using paraphrasing to acknowledge the values and emotions you hear. For example, "It sounds like you have so much on your plate. You have to focus on learning the new literacy program before you think about differentiating 'up.' You value making sure the lesson structure is strong so that you set your students up for success." This acknowledgement shows that you hear the teacher's concerns and recognize what the teacher values in instructional practice. To continue to show that the door is open, you might follow with, "When you are ready, there are some strategies that we could look at together that provide an extra layer of rigor for some of your students who might need it. I'm interested to hear your thoughts about how rigorous the new program is compared to what has been done in the past." In this way, the coach leverages "status" (i.e., SCARF) by acknowledging that the teacher's expert perspective is important.

Reframing through Coaching Moves

Through approaching resistance with curiosity, you may be able to uncover underlying values, fears, and assumptions. Complaints can often be reframed through reflective coaching moves, "Voice the Value" and "Wonder the Worry."

As previously mentioned in this chapter, when teachers voice a complaint, they are communicating what they value. If you can "Voice the Value," this becomes a leverage point for further conversation and next steps. For example, if a teacher complains that the enrichment to be provided to high-potential students is not going to be reflected on state level tests, then the teacher is conveying that they value students demonstrating mastery of learning standards. You might respond with "It seems that you desire for your students to spend their time learning content they are accountable for learning. How are you defining enrichment?" Table 3.6 shows other examples of a teacher's complaint, how the coach might respond to reframe the resistance, and the coaching move associated with the response.

Another approach to reframing resistance is to identify the underlying fear or concern. Perhaps a comment reveals an underlying assumption that you can address in the conversation. We call this "Wonder the Worry." To show you hear their concerns, you could show curiosity using the phrase "I wonder if you are worried . . ." For example, you might ask, "I wonder if you are concerned about how well the enrichment activities align to the state standards. Can we talk about that?" This can lead to a discussion of using pre-assessments to determine

TABLE 3.6
Reframing Resistance from Teacher's Complaints

Teacher Complaint	Coach Response to Reframe	Coaching Move
If I have some students doing different things, then some students are not going to think it's fair.	*You value making sure all students are treated fairly. How do you define differentiation?* (This can open the conversation to discuss equity vs. fairness.)	Voice the Value- The coach acknowledges the value behind the complaint.
I need to stick to the pacing guide, otherwise I might be behind the other teachers on the grade-level team. I can't get off pace.	*I wonder if you are worried that differentiating for high-potential students means that it will take more time. What if there is a way to tier what you are already planning so that you don't have to change your pace? Would you like to look at the pacing guide together?*	Wonder the Worry- The coach uses "I wonder" to mirror the underlying worry or concern. This is followed by a next step question to address the worry.

Source: Adapted from Gross Cheliotes and Reilly (2018).

if students already show mastery of standards or how to add depth and complexity to enrichment in ways that directly align with standards.

Moving Forward

No matter how the conversation goes, at the end of the day, you must remain true to aligning your own beliefs and values to your actions. It is also important to recognize that there will be times that it's best to agree to disagree. In situations like this, you can aim the conversation towards common ground. Perhaps you both hold the same shared goal- for students to learn something new every day.

Sometimes in the spirit of "niceness" it feels easier to avoid a conflict rather than address a teacher's concern head-on. If a teacher expresses a reservation such as "I do not think that tiered assignments are fair," it is not productive to sweep the comment under the rug and say "okay" and hope for the best for next year. Killion et al. note, "When a coach ignores an expressed concern, the individual gets the message that his or her concerns are unimportant or inappropriate and may resist the change" (Killion et al., 2012, p. 77). Acknowledging concerns and listening for values will communicate that the teacher is seen and heard, even if you disagree. It's also okay to admit that you do not know all the answers if a teacher brings up a question you do not know how to address. Responding with "I'm not so sure. Maybe we can find this out" conveys your learner stance as a GT coach. While this requires vulnerability, this vulnerability is what builds authentic relationships and trust.

As a GT coach, remember that you cannot control people; you can only influence the environment and approach their resistance with curiosity. Here, we provide a list of questions as a summary of what's been discussed in this chapter. Consider how the teacher's perception of a situation leads to resistance.

Key questions include:
+ Does the teacher have an opportunity to contribute expertise?
+ Is the teacher treated as a "co-thinker" in this work?
+ Are you valuing the teacher's expertise, or are you unintentionally coming across an expert or advice-giver?
+ Does the teacher see the value in engaging in the coaching conversations with you?
+ Is it worth the "cost" to them (e.g., using planning time to meet with you, making themselves vulnerable to change)?
+ Are aspects of SCARF leveraged in the relationships? Are there any elements of SCARF that are posing as threats (i.e., Status, Certainty, Autonomy, Relatedness, Fairness)?

While we have mentioned to "work with the welcoming" previously in Chapter 2, this does not mean that you should *only* work with the welcoming and completely give up on teachers who are resistant. Instead of throwing in the towel on working with resistors, understand that the teacher is responding out of the beliefs and values they hold. Remember, the coaching mindset assumes that the coach, too, is a learner – this is an opportunity for you to listen and learn about the teacher's perspective through many of the approaches we have shared in this chapter.

We presented the ADKAR model of change in Chapter 1. Through this lens, change happens through awareness, desire, knowledge, ability, and reinforcement. Teachers are at different points of preparedness for change. Since the first step is awareness, consider that many teachers will continue to benefit from the information you share in PLCs, team meetings, or other workshop opportunities, even if they do not engage with follow-up coaching. This awareness could eventually lead to a desire to change practices over time.

You can also open doors for future conversations by asking what we call, the Awareness question:

> *Awareness question: When you think about challenging every student in your classroom, what are the obstacles that get in the way?*

This question (adapted from Toll, 2005) could be asked as part of PLC meetings or in one-on-one conversations. It conveys a presumption of positive intent because it considers that teachers have their own goals to pursue and acknowledges their own capabilities. As teachers reflect on their own teaching practices, this question can ignite the *awareness* and *desire* to grow in their knowledge and practice of teaching gifted and high-potential students. Creating this awareness is addressed further in Chapter 4.

The reality is that you will have a handful of teachers who want to engage with you in coaching while you have a handful who won't. It is easy to feel discouraged by a lack of buy-in or a lack of awareness around teaching GT students. A key to resilience is understanding what you can control and not control. By accepting what you cannot control, it can bring a sense of relief in knowing how to expend energy and effort. After reflecting on the extent to which you have created a welcoming SCARF-based space and after considering where teachers are in their awareness and desire to bring change to their instructional practices, plan your next steps in supporting those who are ready.

Reflection Questions

1. In reflecting on your own counterproductive listening behaviors, how might this heightened awareness benefit you in future GT coaching conversations? How will you remain mindful of the intention behind your listening behaviors to move coaching conversations forward in a positive manner?
2. By engaging in reflective practice with a classroom teacher through presuming positive intent, in what ways does this approach build upon the TEAM (Trust, Engage, Align, Maintain) framework? How might this alignment create a stronger context for GT coaching practices?
3. In what ways do the Green, Yellow, and Red light levels of coaching respect teacher autonomy? When working through the Yellow light level, how might you continue to leverage the expertise of the classroom teacher while co-constructing new knowledge?
4. As you consider why teachers resist coaching, what connections do you make with your own experiences?

References

Bohm, D., & Rickles, D. (2014). *On dialogue*. Routledge.

Costa, A. L, & Garmston, R. J. (2015). *Cognitive coaching: Developing self-directed leaders and learners* (3rd ed.). Rowman & Littlefield.

Gross Cheliotes, L.M. & Reilly, M.F. (2018). *Coaching conversations: Transforming your school one conversation at a time* (2nd ed.). Corwin Press.

Kee, K., Anderson, K., Dearing, V., Harris, E., & Shuster, F. (2010). *Results coaching: The new essentials for school leaders*. Corwin.

Perkins, D. (2003). *King Arthur's round table: How collaborative conversations create smart organizations*. Wiley & Sons.

Toll, C.A. (2005). *The literacy coach's survival guide: Essential question and practical answers*. International Reading Association.

Chapter 4

The Coaching Circuit

Set a Purpose

In this chapter, we explain a step-by-step approach for guiding a conversation towards a teacher established goal in the GT Coaching Circuit. This chapter specifically focuses on "Set a Purpose" as it relates to the overall Collaborative Process Model introduced in Chapter 1. We provide a structure for setting the stage for coaching, using third point tools to drive dialogue, establishing a need for coaching through igniting awareness, and guiding a teacher to create a student-focused goal. At the end of this chapter, we provide coaching notes for this stage (Resource 4.1: Coaching Notes: Set a Purpose; available at www.routledge.com/9781032375144). Appendix B shows a sample scenario of a teacher and GT coach engaging in a full coaching circuit. Refer to it throughout this chapter to see how the stage "Set a Purpose" unfolds in dialogue.

Setting the Stage

Before engaging in the coaching circuit, it's a good idea to have an informal one-on-one meeting to get to know the teacher on a personal level and establish a shared understanding about coaching. During this meeting (perhaps over a cup of coffee or tea), you may discuss what your role is, especially if it has recently shifted from that of a GT teacher/specialist to a GT coach. You can clarify any

DOI: 10.4324/9781003340560-5

misconceptions about your role and share that you are learning along the way as well. This is also a good opportunity to convey the vision and goals of the GT program as it relates to talent development, specifically that you are working to bring elements of gifted pedagogy into the regular education classroom and expose *all* students to critical thinking, creative thinking, open inquiry, etc. You might also share that one of the goals of the school is to provide differentiated instruction within the classroom, and you can support the teacher in selecting and adapting resources to make this happen. Sharing your appreciation for the teacher's willingness to collaborate with you and expressing any part of your own vulnerability will go a long way in establishing a meaningful relationship.

This conversation can also involve getting to know the teacher by asking questions and sharing about your own educational experiences without coming across as "the expert." Remember, we want to keep in mind how *status* affects relationships (i.e., SCARF). The questions that follow are related to each part of the TEAM framework for establishing a shared understanding of the coaching process. The questions do not have to be asked in this order, and of course, not all questions have to be asked. The main goal of the initial conversation is to make sure the teacher feels comfortable working with you and providing a positive rationale for the coaching relationship.

Trust

+ What brought you to the field of education?
+ How long have you been teaching?
+ What do you enjoy doing when you are not teaching?
+ What are your greatest fears about engaging in coaching?
+ What are your greatest hopes about the coaching relationship?
+ What barriers have you encountered (in teaching)?

Engage their Expertise

+ What are your strengths in teaching?
+ What units of study do you look forward to teaching this year?
+ What's your favorite content to teach?
+ What do you know about your student's readiness levels? Interests? Funds of knowledge?

Align

+ What are your beliefs about gifted learners?
+ What are your core values?
+ My core values are_____. Because I value_____, I try to _____.

Maintain

+ Is there anything you can share with me that will help me support you?
+ Is there anything we need to change in working together?
+ What are you most excited about in this experience?

Shared Understanding

+ What expectations do you have for this experience? What do you hope to achieve?
+ Share any norms (e.g., Let's decide how we will meet. Perhaps we can meet every week/two weeks for 20 minutes. . .).
+ Share role of a coach (i.e., a supporter for the teacher's growth).
+ How might we keep our focus on providing opportunities for students to show and grow their strengths and talents?

Third Point Tools

Dialogue is at the heart of GT coaching. Dialogue centered on data or other sources (rather than on the teacher) can be a less-threatening way to engage in purposeful conversations. Third point tools aid in this process and are exactly as they sound, a "third point," or discussion point. Third point tools focus the reflective dialogue on items such as informational documents, student work samples, videos, or other artifacts. By guiding a classroom teacher through examining a third point tool, the focus is on the document rather than the person. This removes potential threats to a teacher's personal instructional practices but continues to allow for reflection. Table 4.1 provides a list of possible third point tools that are easily used within the GT coaching context.

TABLE 4.1
Third Point Tool Examples

+ Professional learning materials	+ PLC documents
+ Above grade level standards	+ NAGC (2019) Gifted Programming Standards
+ Data meeting resources	
+ Student work samples	+ Above grade level standards
+ Teacher/student-created rubrics	+ Teaching videos
+ Case studies	+ Curriculum map/Scope and sequence

Third point tools serve as "conversation starters" that lead to a teacher engaging with and having "buy-in" to the coaching process. In turn, the use of third point tools often shine a light on a teacher's area of need which continues to inform the goal-setting process.

Set a Purpose

So, you are ready to have your first coaching session. It's important to remember, "You don't have to be great to start, you just have to start to be great!" (Zig Ziglar Quotes, n.d.). If you are new to coaching, remember that much of what you do requires stepping out of your comfort zone and having the courage to tackle new challenges. In taking the first step in the coaching circuit, you and the teacher must know the purpose of the process. The start of any meaningful journey must include a shared understanding of the main aim for the teacher's growth. If you have not already established this shared understanding in a pre-meeting, it is important to do so now.

As we explain the steps that follow, please keep in mind that coaching in the real world is not a step-by-step linear process. We present the GT Coaching Circuit only as a flexible framework for understanding important components to facilitating reflective growth. We love the phrase – *structure promotes function*. Guides such as this can establish certainty (an important component of SCARF) for what happens in the coaching process. We have talked to a number of individuals in coaching roles who have shared that it takes a long time to figure out what to do as a coach. So, we developed this structure to pave a path forward, based on the Collaborative Process Model (Mofield & Phelps, 2020): Set a Purpose, Plan and Act, Reflect.

In the first stage of the circuit sequence, the coaching conversation leads to exploring a focus question. As we explained in Chapter 2, a coach is a "vehicle" that serves to facilitate movement of a teacher from their current state to an aspirational state. In a nutshell, the stage "Set a Purpose" involves opening an awareness of the current reality and considering a more ideal reality (Knight, 2018). This is quite different from simply asking, "Hey there! How's your week? What do you want to work on today?" While it is possible that this could lead to a goal, it would not allow for the opportunity for a teacher to have self-awareness of what is currently working and not working.

This stage is situated around the components of "Awareness" and "Desire" from the ADKAR change model (explained in Chapter 1). Individuals do not change without an awareness or desire to do so. This process described in this stage builds buy-in by leveraging a teacher's autonomy and keeping the attention on the teacher's needs and goals as related to student outcomes.

Evaluate Need

So, how do we craft questions in such a way to build this self-awareness? What is the teacher's point of reference for their current reality as it relates to identifying and teaching gifted and high-potential students? How can you leverage your role as a GT coach to build capacity and awareness of the teacher's current practices?

First, the GT coach must guide the teacher to evaluate their "need" established by their current reality. There are multiple ways to start this process.

1. *Follow-Up on Professional Learning*

    Take the opportunity to start a conversation after a recent professional learning experience. For example, you may have provided a one-hour training session about infusing creativity with content instruction to the school faculty. In a conversation with the teacher, you may ask, "As you think about providing opportunities for students to use creative thinking, on a scale from 1–10, how well do you think students have opportunities to think creatively about the content you are teaching?" This allows the teacher to reflect on their current reality and become self-aware of their own skills. As shown in Resource 4.1 (end of the chapter), you could follow up with other reflective questions such as "What makes you say 4 instead of a 1? What would it take to for you to feel more confident in this area?" These questions (inspired from Knight, 2018) open pathways for you as a coach to hear how the teacher has interpreted the information presented at the professional learning session and offer entry points for focusing next steps on developing a specific student-centered goal focused on gifted/high-potential students.

2. *Use a Third Point Tool to Create an Awareness of Need*

    Focusing the conversation on a specific document can reduce the threat of focusing directly on a teacher's behavior. For example, you may provide an article for teachers to read about behaviors and characteristics of twice-exceptional students or a handout highlighting a specific thinking framework (e.g., Bloom's taxonomy). The coaching dialogue can focus on the document rather than directly on the teacher. You could ask "How is Bloom's taxonomy beneficial for planning instruction for all students?

How might it be incorporated with advanced content, specifically for gifted/high-potential students?"

3. *Use a Teacher Self-Assessment to Identify an Area of Need*

    Providing teachers an opportunity to self-assess their own instructional practice is another way to evaluate need. Resource 4.2, Teacher Self-Assessment of Instructional Practice, provides a short self-assessment tool adapted from the NAGC (2019) Gifted Programming Standards. As teachers personally reflect on their own instructional practice in regard to meeting the needs of gifted and high-potential learners, they are able to identify areas that could be strengthened. Depending on each individual teacher's need, the coach might engage the teacher in dialogue by stating, "I see you do not feel as confident in [this area], how might that be impacting your instruction?"

Teacher Self-Assessment of Instructional Practice

Directions: Below is a list of statements focused on instructional practices associated with meeting the needs of gifted/high-potential learners. As you consider your own instructional practice, indicate your current level of confidence for each statement.

1. I use above grade level standards to expand, enrich, and/or accelerate differentiated content.

1	2	3	4	5	6	7	8	9	10
Not Confident At All									Highly Confident

2. I consider students' strengths, interests, and backgrounds to develop differentiated content.

1	2	3	4	5	6	7	8	9	10
Not Confident At All									Highly Confident

3. I regularly use pre-assessments to develop differentiated content.

1	2	3	4	5	6	7	8	9	10
Not Confident At All									Highly Confident

4. I consistently integrate opportunities for psychosocial development within instructional design.

1	2	3	4	5	6	7	8	9	10
Not Confident At All									Highly Confident

5. I integrate multiple perspectives as related to the real-world within instructional design.

1	2	3	4	5	6	7	8	9	10
Not Confident At All									Highly Confident

6. I select, adapt, and use evidence-based strategies to differentiate for gifted/high-potential learners.

1	2	3	4	5	6	7	8	9	10
Not Confident At All									Highly Confident

7. I provide opportunities for students to explore, develop, or research in areas of talent or interest.

1	2	3	4	5	6	7	8	9	10
Not Confident At All									Highly Confident

8. I use models of inquiry to engage students in critical thinking, creative thinking, and problem-solving.

1	2	3	4	5	6	7	8	9	10
Not Confident At All									Highly Confident

9. I use metacognitive models that encourage self-regulated learning.

1	2	3	4	5	6	7	8	9	10
Not Confident At All									Highly Confident

10. I scaffold as a means to differentiate "up" or to provide access to talent development opportunities.

1	2	3	4	5	6	7	8	9	10
Not Confident At All									Highly Confident

11. I use flexible grouping within differentiated learning.

1	2	3	4	5	6	7	8	9	10
Not Confident At All									Highly Confident

12. I hold high expectations and encourage students to think like disciplinarians.

1	2	3	4	5	6	7	8	9	10
Not Confident At All									Highly Confident

13. I regularly use differentiated formative assessments that guide my instructional decisions.

1	2	3	4	5	6	7	8	9	10
Not Confident At All									Highly Confident

14. I use above grade level assessments to measure academic growth.

1	2	3	4	5	6	7	8	9	10
Not Confident At All									Highly Confident

15. I provide opportunities for students to set personal goals and monitor their own learning.

1	2	3	4	5	6	7	8	9	10
Not Confident At All									Highly Confident

16. I provide opportunities for students to engage in transfer of learning across different contexts.

1	2	3	4	5	6	7	8	9	10
Not Confident At All									Highly Confident

17. I provide opportunities for students to reflect on learning and how it connects to their own lives.

1	2	3	4	5	6	7	8	9	10
Not Confident At All									Highly Confident

Note: Adapted from NAGC (2019) Gifted Programing Standards

4. *Use Student Data (also a Third Point Tool)*
   Consider the following questions to discuss the current reality of student learning:
   + What does the data show us about student readiness levels?
   + How does the data connect to what you know about student strengths?
   + What does the data reveal about what students need to progress in their learning?
   + How does this student work show evidence of creative thinking? Critical thinking?

5. *Use the Awareness Question*
   As we previously described in Chapter 3, the aim of asking this question is to address barriers to challenging gifted/high-potential students. Asking this question presumes positive intent because it presupposes that the teacher already values the aim of challenging every student. [Note, this question is adapted from Toll (2005) from her work with literacy coaching, but applied here to gifted context.]

   Awareness question: When you think about challenging every student in your classroom, what are the obstacles that get in the way?

   A discussion of this obstacle will pave the way for a discussion about the teacher's goal.

Establish a Goal

This part of the coaching circuit involves guiding a teacher to establish a goal, consider criteria of success, and understand the baseline for where students are in relation to the goal.

Student-Centered Goals: What Do You Want Students to Think and Do?

Now it is time to guide the teacher in establishing a goal to focus on during the coaching circuit. After listening to the teacher's own evaluation of need (through a third point tool, follow-up from professional learning, student data, or the awareness question), paraphrase some of what was shared to convey committed listening. For example, if the teacher has shared, "I know that I should be challenging my gifted students to engage in more complex problem solving, but I just don't know how," the coach might follow up with "It sounds like you want students to explore complex problems, is that right?" From here, you can guide the teacher to consider how this focus will impact student learning. For example, you might ask,

+ "What might this lead to for your high-potential students?"
+ "What do you want your students to ultimately be able to learn by engaging in more complex problem solving?"

Through this dialogue, you can co-think with the teacher to establish a student-centered goal. If the goal is written as "I will infuse problem-solving in student tasks" the focus is on the teacher's behavior. If it is worded as "Students will show evidence of problem solving through real-world issues" the next stages of the coaching circuit can be centered on how students *learn*, not how teachers teach. How we frame the goal influences how it is achieved.

Examples of student-centered goals that relate well to the contexts of GT coaching are included here:

+ Students will collaborate on tasks that allow for open inquiry.
+ Students will evaluate, synthesize, and analyze during a Socratic seminar.
+ Students will think and write like a scientist.
+ Students will engage in peer and self-reflection on their own growth.
+ Students will build arguments in multiple forms.
+ Students will use strategic thinking and reasoning during class discussions.
+ Students will use creative thinking while engaged in learning tasks.
+ Students will transfer their learning to new contexts.

We emphasize that the goal should be student-centered and come from the *teacher's* desire for growth. Again, this respects their own autonomy within this process (i.e., SCARF). The goal should lead to exploring how the teacher's actions affect student learning. If the conversation seems to be about a teacher describing their own behavior, continue to ask questions so that the conversation leads to what *students* will know, do, or understand. Because the coaching circuit revolves around meeting the goal, it is important to write down the goal on the coaching notes so that the GT coach and teacher can refer to it throughout the coaching circuit.

Vision of Success: What does this look like?

Depending on the teacher's readiness level, you could ask, "What would it look like if students. . .(goal)? You may jot down a few ideas that would help establish a clear vision of success. However, the teacher may or may not yet have this vision or understanding of what it would look like. If this is the case, there are opportunities in the next stage to provide further clarity on criteria for success, and this can be revisited.

For example, if the goal is for students to think like a disciplinarian in Language Arts, discussing "what this might look like" will pave the way for establishing criteria for success. Through this conversation as co-thinking partners, you may arrive at a list that students would be able to show in their work such as:

+ Analyze the structure of a text and how it promotes meaning.
+ Make connections to other texts.
+ Analyze the author's craft.
+ Compare the author's style to other authors.

This not only establishes a vision of success, it also establishes guiding criteria for next steps in the coaching circuit.

Baseline: Where are They Now?

If it has not already been discussed, it is important to ask where students are in relation to this goal already. This establishes a baseline that can be revisited later in the coaching circuit (in Stage 3 – Reflect, see Chapter 6) when the conversation focuses on the extent to which the goal has been met. You may ask "Where are your students currently in relation to (goal)? How do you know?" The criteria outlined in creating a "vision for success" previously described can also be used here as a lens for understanding students' starting points. This can open doors for opportunities to discuss how you might assess student learning and growth.

Explore Ideas

After establishing a goal, develop a focus question to start exploring ideas. We suggest using the phrases "In what ways might. . . ." or "How might . . ." to frame the conversation. For example, by asking, "How might students show more high-level thinking in tiered assignments?" this sets the stage for exploring multiple options to address this goal. Examples of focus questions might include:

+ How might students collaborate on tasks that allow for open inquiry?
+ How might students evaluate, synthesize, and analyze during a Socratic seminar?
+ How might students think and write like scientists?
+ How might students engage in peer and self-reflection on their own growth?
+ How might students build arguments in multiple forms?
+ How might students use strategic thinking and reasoning during class discussions?

+ How might students use creative thinking while engaged in advanced learning tasks?

At this point in the conversation, you might begin to explore what the teacher already knows. To respect autonomy, you might ask, "What ideas do you have already?" Here, you can listen for the potential in possibilities and remember to apply principles of paraphrasing and reflective feedback in the conversation. For example, "You really seem to value student choice. That will be impactful to your students' motivation." Listen for the possibilities and leverage them throughout the conversation.

It might be that the teacher does not have many ideas, which is why they want to focus on this particular goal. Instead of going into "advice mode," we suggest moving into the Yellow light level (as described in Chapter 3) and asking to partner with the teacher in brainstorming a number of ideas. For example, "Would you like to brainstorm ideas together?" This sets the stage for next steps in the coaching circuit (see Chapter 5).

Summary

Overall, this stage addresses the "awareness" and "desire" aspects of the ADKAR change model. Teachers gain an awareness by reflecting on recent professional learning, a third point tool, student data, or specific barriers that are at play when challenging all learners in the classroom. The desire to participate in coaching is further established by the development of a teacher-selected goal. We emphasize this goal is directly tied to the *teacher's* desire to focus on a particular student outcome, not the coach's. The coach's role is to dialogue with the teacher to clarify the goal, establish a vision for success, and understand where students already are in relation to the goal. Once the goal is established, the coach and teacher explore a number of options, guided by a student-centered focus question.

Reflection Questions

1. How do the components within this circuit stage relate back to the components of SCARF?
2. What third point tools might you use in coaching conversations?
3. How does the Set a Purpose stage establish buy-in for the teacher?
4. Practice through role-play this stage with a colleague. Reflect on your emotions and the emotions of the teacher. What are areas that are uncomfortable for you? How can this awareness prepare you for your first coaching sessions?

RESOURCE 4.1
Coaching Notes: Set a Purpose

Set a Purpose	Coaching Notes	Coaching Prompts
Establish a Student-Focused Goal		+ *What do you want to focus on?*
Evaluate Need		+ *You value_____. It's exciting to see____.*
–Determine Need: *As you think about the gifted/high-potential students in your classroom*		+ *What would happen if____?*
+ *What do you know about their readiness levels? Strengths?*		+ *I'm curious about that . . .*
+ *What do they need to progress in their learning? How do you know?*		+ *Tell me more . . .*
+ *What are their next steps in learning?*		+ *So, in other words____? Is that right?*
+ *On a scale from 1–10, how well do you think____? Why did you not say 1? What would it take to for you to feel more confident?*		+ *So, you are saying____.*
+ *When you think about challenging every student in the classroom, what gets in the way?*		+ *You are wanting students to . . .*
	Goal:	
Establish Goal		
+ *Goal- What are you wanting students to do and understand?*		
+ *Criteria- What might this look like?*		
+ *Baseline- Where are students already in relation to this goal?*		
Explore Ideas		
–Create a Focus Question		
+ *In what ways might____? How might students____?-Brainstorm*		
+ *What ideas do you have already?*		
+ *Would you like to brainstorm ideas together?*		

References

Knight, J. (2018). *The impact cycle: What instructional coaches should do to foster powerful improvements in teaching.* Corwin.

Mofield, E., & Phelps, V. (2020). *Collaboration, coteaching, and coaching in gifted education: Sharing strategies to support gifted learners.* Prufrock Press.

National Association for Gifted Children. (2019). 2019 Pre-K–Grade 12 Gifted Programming Standards. http://www.nagc.org/sites/default/files/standards/Intro%202019%20Programming%20Standards.pdf.

Toll, C.A. (2005). *The literacy coach's survival guide: Essential question and practical answers.* International Reading Association.

Zig Ziglar Quotes. (n.d.). BrainyQuote.com. https://www.brainyquote.com/quotes/zig_ziglar_617778.

Chapter 5

The Coaching Circuit

Plan and Act

In this chapter, we explain a flexible structure for the GT coach and teacher to select an instructional strategy, determine how to use the strategy within the classroom context, and implement it within instruction. This chapter specifically focuses on "Plan and Act," the second stage in the GT Coaching Circuit. The co-thinking and co-action involved in the Plan and Act stage focuses intentionally on *how students learn* vs. how the teacher instructs. Remaining student-centered is integral in not only creating student agency, but also improving student outcomes. In this stage of the coaching circuit, you and your collaborating teacher will:

+ Select which strategy best supports the desired student outcomes.
+ Plan for co-action on next steps to work toward the goal.
+ Address how the teacher will independently implement the strategy to engage and challenge gifted and high-potential learners.

At the end of this chapter, we have provided Resource 5.1: Coaching Notes: Plan and Act (downloadable at www.routledge.com/9781032375144) to guide and support teachers through this stage. Continue to refer to Appendix B to see the sample scenario of a teacher and GT coach selecting and learning a strategy through "Plan and Act."

DOI: 10.4324/9781003340560-6

Select a Strategy

In Stage 2 of the coaching circuit, the GT coach and teacher begin to choose a strategy to implement. In addressing the focus question from Stage 1, "How might students___" the teacher and coach may brainstorm a number of ideas. These options may consist of specific strategies, models, and/or frameworks. Frameworks might consist of common language (e.g., depth, complexity, advanced content, creativity) associated with a school district's gifted mission statement, or it might also include a particular curriculum model that provides clear guidance for instructional decision making.

With the brainstormed list completed, the GT coach and teacher begin to explore *which* strategy is most beneficial in targeting gifted/high-potential students' needs in relation to the goal. The ABC's of Differentiation (adapted from Mofield, 2023; see Table 5.1) are ways to apply vertical differentiation (differentiating "up") for gifted/high-potential students. By using the ABC's in the coaching conversation, the collaborating teacher can select a strategy with an awareness to integrate advanced content, build buy-in, create opportunities for challenge, and determine scaffolds that provide access to accelerated content.

Depending on the experience of the teacher, the GT coach might also need to provide an overview of any unfamiliar strategies. This is often the case when the teacher has asked the GT coach for strategy suggestions. In these cases, ensure that the teacher has a foundational understanding of each listed strategy,

TABLE 5.1

ABCs of Differentiation

Advance the Content	Build the Buy-In	Create Challenge	Determine Scaffolds
+ Accelerate content + Advanced resources + Advanced vocabulary + Content-expert thinking + Above grade level standards	+ Choices + Agency + Funds of Knowledge + Real-world connection + Create task value tied to identity, interest, future	+ Open inquiry + Depth and complexity + Creative thinking + Critical thinking + High-level thinking + Abstract thinking + Critical thinking + Transfer + Metacognition	+ Sentence stems + Graphic organizers + Visual Aids + Prompts + Checklists + Chunking

Adapted from Mofield (2023). *Vertical differentiation for gifted, advanced, and high-potential students: 25 strategies to stretch student thinking.* Routledge.

including its purpose (e.g., enhances critical thinking, adds more depth) and how it relates to the teacher's goal. In Appendix C, we provide the GT Toolkit of Strategies and Thinking Models which highlights models, strategies, and resources for vertical differentiation. This toolkit is meant to serve as a "go-to" guide to support GT coaches as they engage teachers in coaching conversations. Additionally, Appendix D provides a general overview of various differentiation features with examples of practice.

Narrowing the Focus

As the GT coach and teacher select the appropriate strategy, the GT coach might begin by stating, "Think about your student-focused goal and the possibilities of how students might be able to demonstrate that goal. Which strategy might best guide students in this learning?" If, for example, the teacher's goal is focused on integrating creative thinking into learning, the brainstormed list might include the four dimensions of creativity: fluency, flexibility, originality, and elaboration (Guilford, 1986), SCAMPER, or arts integration through STEAM (i.e., Science, Technology, Engineering, Arts, Mathematics).

As different strategies are considered, the GT coach should refrain from leading the teacher to a specific strategy. In doing so, it is nearly impossible to learn more about the teacher's thought process. Think of these coaching conversations as a way to gain greater insight into how to best support the teacher in instructional decision-making through the GT Coaching Circuit, much like a formative assessment within a classroom. The teacher should have the final decision about which strategy best supports the established goal. In providing this level of autonomy, the GT coach is able to leverage the teacher's professional discretion of determining best practices for their classroom (Knight, 2019).

Considerations for Strategy Selection

When choosing a strategy, the teacher should consider its purpose and impact on student learning. The GT Toolkit (see Appendix C) provides a quick reference for the *purpose* of various strategies. This toolkit shows *why* and *how* strategies are often used to stretch gifted and high-potential students in their learning.

Consider Purpose of the Strategy

First, discuss if the selected strategy aligns with the goal established in Stage 1. The GT coach might begin by asking, "How are the desired student outcomes aligned with the purpose of the strategy?" The GT coach can then follow-up with additional questions focused on how each strategy addresses the needs of gifted/high-potential learners. These questions might include:

+ What aspects of the strategy provide the most authentic (i.e., natural, unforced) alignment with the desired outcome/instructional objective for gifted and high-potential learners?
+ In what ways might above grade level standards be integrated with the strategy?
+ In knowing the classroom context, how does the strategy promote academic achievement and student growth among gifted/high-potential learners?

Depending on the needs of the teacher and the student-focused goal, the GT coach might also guide the teacher in evaluating how specific strategies incorporate the desired student outcomes. For example, if the teacher's goal is tied to critical thinking and/or creative thinking, the GT coach and teacher could focus more deeply on how the selected strategy provides opportunities for these outcomes by using. Resource 5.2 (downloadable at www.routledge. com/9781032375144).

Critical Thinking and Creative Thinking Considerations for Strategy Selection

Directions: Choose a specific strategy and explore how it might present students with an opportunity to engage in critical thinking and/or creative thinking. For each marked area, include any notes specifically tied to the targeted instructional objectives.

Strategy:

Opportunities to Engage in Critical Thinking	
Students examine missing parts. Notes:	Students make judgments. Notes:
Students question arguments. Notes:	Students judge credibility and evidence. Notes:
Students look at other points of view. Notes:	Students examine how parts work together as a whole. Notes:
Students make cause-effect statements. Notes:	Students explain effects of effects. Notes:
Students discuss interactions between elements. Notes:	Students explain contributions of s on y. Notes:

Opportunities to Engage in Creative Thinking	
Students develop alternative solutions. Notes:	Students make connections between two seemingly unrelated things. Notes:
Students redesign or rearrange for a specific purpose. Notes:	Students develop a new approach or plan. Notes:

Adapted from Mofield (2023)

Beyond addressing how the strategy aligns with the identified learning objective and targeted standards, the GT coach and teacher co-think through how the strategy also provides opportunities for all students to be challenged through their zone of proximal development (Vygotsky, 1978). Likewise, students' needs, backgrounds, and past experiences should be taken into consideration. For example, if a lesson's focus is on biomimicry and the class has no background knowledge on this topic, asking students to partake in a conversation through de Bono's (2016) Six Thinking Hats would not be the best instructional choice. Likewise, if a particular class does not understand the principles of accountable talk, it would not be purposeful to move directly into a Socratic seminar focused on accelerated content without first developing the key skills necessary to implement this strategy with integrity. When choosing a strategy, the GT coach should continue to integrate purpose, timing, and context into the strategy selection conversation (Fisher et al., 2016).

Consider Impact on Student Learning

As the GT coach and teacher evaluate which strategy would be the best option in working toward the student-focused goal, it is beneficial to examine the impact that various strategies have on student achievement. One approach to doing so is to consider effect sizes. In short, an effect size of $d = 1.0$ signifies an increase of one standard deviation on the outcome, and $d = 1.0$ is regarded as a "large, blatantly obvious, and grossly perceptible difference" (Cohen, 1988). This means that as we examine effect sizes, anything over 0.40 should be considered roughly as having an impact of one year's worth of academic growth on student achievement (Hattie, 2012). Table 5.2 provides examples of effect sizes for various instructional strategies (Hattie, 2017).

In recognizing the degree to which different strategies impact student achievement, the GT coach and teacher might explore these strategies further. Possible questions include:

+ How might the strategy provide opportunities for acceleration based on student need?
+ How does the strategy provide opportunities to engage in problem-solving, transfer of knowledge, and/or deep discussion?
+ How does the strategy provide opportunities for students to make connections (within and across content)?

By engaging in this dialogue, the teacher develops a greater knowledge of strategies. As signified in the ADKAR Model (Hiatt, 2006), the GT coach is then able to strengthen the teacher's "ability" to evaluate and differentiate between which contexts each strategy might be most beneficial. Many of these various

TABLE 5.2
Effect Size as Related to Various Strategies

Strategy	Effect Size (ES)
Jigsaw	1.20
Strategy to Integrate with Prior Knowledge	0.93
Transfer Strategies	0.86
Classroom Discussion	0.82
Scaffolding	0.82
Summarization	0.79
Planning and Prediction	0.76
Elaboration and Organization	0.75
Elaboration and Reflection	0.75
Feedback	0.70
Acceleration	0.68
Problem-Solving Teaching	0.68
Concept-Mapping	0.64
Direct Instruction	0.60
Metacognitive Strategies	0.60

Adapted from Hattie (2017).

considerations could be prioritized and weighted differently depending on the teacher-selected goal and classroom context.

Tool Template: How to Use the Strategy

At this point, you might have teachers who feel confident with the selected strategy and are eager to begin co-planning. For those who are still learning the strategy, it is important to make sure they have a clear understanding of how to implement the strategy. While we have already referenced the GT Toolkit (see Appendix C) as a resource to guide the strategy selection process, here we introduce the Tool Template (see Resource 5.3; downloadable at www. routledge.com/9781032375144). This resource provides a flexible structure to explicitly outline the steps of *how* the selected strategy is implemented. In addition to building capacity in the collaborating teacher, it also serves to activate the next stages of the co-planning process.

The Tool Template is structured in the same manner (i.e., *what, why, how*) as the GT Toolkit. Not only does this provide the GT coach with a consistent alignment within coaching conversations, it also keeps the purpose of the strategy at the forefront of the instructional decision-making process. This resource is meant to be completed as part of a coaching conversation focused on the key steps involved in implementing the strategy, as well as a space to note any needed materials/resources.

At the bottom of the Tool Template, the ABCs of Differentiation are also included to signify additional opportunities to address the needs of gifted/high-potential learners. The Tool Template is not meant to be a lesson plan. Its purpose is to provide a means through which the GT coach and teacher can systematically focus through a step-by-step approach for *how* the strategy is meant to be delivered with integrity. Keep in mind that effective outcomes are the result of effective implementation of strategies (Knight, 2019), so without a clear understanding of the strategy, effective implementation is rarely achieved. Table 5.3 provides an example of how the Tool Template might be completed for use with the Double Fishbone strategy (see Appendix C).

The "What"	The "Why"
Strategy:	Purpose:

The "How"

Key Steps:

Materials/Resources:

Advance the Content	Build the Buy-In	Create Challenge	Determine Scaffolds
+ Accelerate content + Advanced resources + Advanced vocabulary + Content-expert thinking + Above grade level standards	+ Choices + Agency + Funds of Knowledge + Real-world connection + Create task value tied to identity, interest, future	+ Open inquiry + Depth/complexity + Creative thinking + High-level thinking + Abstract thinking + Critical thinking + Transfer + Metacognition	+ Sentence stems + Graphic organizers + Visual Aids + Prompts + Checklists + Chunking

Adapted from Mofield (2023).

TABLE 5.3
Tool Template Example

The "What" Strategy: Double Fishbone	The "Why" Purpose: To analyze cause and effect relationships

The "How"
Key Steps:

1) Students write issue, problem, or situation in the center square
2) Students complete "fishbones" to the left of the center square with direct and indirect causes, or influences, of the problem
3) Students complete "fishbones" to the right of the center square with multiple effects of the problem, including short-term/long-term effects and positive/negative effects
4) Through differentiating "up," students create additional "fishbones" stemming from existing fishbones, to signify causes of causes or effects of effects

Materials/Resources: Fishbone Template

Advance the Content	Build the Buy-In	Create Challenge	Determine Scaffolds
+ Accelerate content + Advanced resources + Advanced vocabulary + Content-expert thinking + Above grade level standards	+ Choices + Agency + Funds of Knowledge + Real-world connection + Create task value tied to identity, interest, future	+ Open inquiry + Depth and complexity + Creative thinking + High-level thinking + Abstract thinking + Critical thinking + Transfer + Metacognition	+ Sentence stems + Graphic organizers + Visual Aids + Prompts + Checklists + Chunking

Adapted from Mofield (2023).

The GT Instructional Blueprint: Considering Classroom Context

Once the teacher feels confident in the key steps of the strategy, it is now time to delve deeper into how the strategy can best be implemented within the context of the specific classroom. In any given classroom, it is realistic to acknowledge that there will be diverse learning needs, including twice-exceptional students, RCLED (i.e., racially, culturally, linguistically, economically diverse) students, and students with multiple readiness levels, various interests, and values. These are just a few factors that impact how the strategy is delivered and received within a particular context. When co-thinking through this process, the GT coach might simply ask, "How might this strategy be used with your students?" or "How do you think you might modify this strategy with your students when working toward your goal?" (adapted from Knight, 2018).

The GT Instructional Blueprint and Guide (see Resource 5.4; downloadable at www.routledge.com/9781032375144) is designed to provide flexibility in co-thinking how a strategy can be purposefully implemented within any given context through the lens of high leverage practices, student agency, and access points for learning. The Blueprint can be also used later in co-planning, as it is a versatile space to design next steps for instruction, much like a blueprint provides the space to design a dream home (e.g., doors for access, height of countertops, room arrangement). Similarly, the GT Toolkit (Appendix C), as referenced earlier, provides the tools for constructing new knowledge, and the Tool Template becomes a specialized tool to refine understanding of a specific strategy. When we think about how all of these resources work together to support coaching conversations, we are then able to recognize how the coaching circuit, itself, provides the power to ignite potential in the process.

Keep in mind that each coaching conversation is different, and many goals may not align with every aspect that is outlined within this resource. The goal is to provide a breadth and depth of support for GT coaching which can be appropriately leveraged in regard to any teacher's specific goal and needs.

GT Instructional Blueprint

Student-Focused Goal:

Selected Strategy:

Purpose:

How might this strategy be applied in your classroom context with *your* students?
When considering the ABC's of Differentiation, how will HLPs, access points, and agency further support/extend student learning?

High Leverage Practices	Agency	Access Points

GT Instructional Blueprint

How might this strategy be applied in your classroom context with *your* students?
When considering the ABC's of Differentiation, how will HLPs, access points, and agency further support/extend student learning?

High Leverage Practices	Agency	Access Points
+ How might gifted and high-potential learners grow and develop *interpersonal skills with peers*? (HLP9) + How might this strategy provide opportunities to *adapt curriculum tasks and materials* to address gifted and high-potential learners? (HLP13) + How might students use *metacognitive thinking* as they learn advanced content? (HLP14) + Given the context of your class, what *scaffolded supports* could be integrated to support students in their zone of proximal development? (HLP15) + How might *flexible grouping* be integrated within this strategy to best address student readiness levels? (HLP17) + How will gifted and high-potential learners feel *actively engaged* in their learning throughout this strategy? (HLP18) + In what ways are gifted and high-potential students able to *generalize new learning* through this strategy? (HLP21)	+ How will students connect conceptual understandings to their personal life? + In knowing students' diverse backgrounds, in what ways might students connect their interests, future goals, and/or identities to new learning? + In what ways does this strategy or learning experience provide students with an opportunity to take responsibility and ownership of their learning? + How does this strategy allow students to take action or make a contribution?	+ What previous experience do your students have with the strategy and/or content we have listed? How might this past experience impact how they connect to the new learning associated with your chosen goal? + In what ways are students able to make connections between the focused content and their funds of knowledge/life experiences? + Given the differentiation needs of your classroom, how might you modify the strategy to provide all students in your classroom to work in their zone of proximal development? + In knowing students' current skills and previous exposure to varied instructional strategies, how does this strategy provide entry points to access and engage with advanced content? + In analyzing the pre-assessment data of the unit of study, how does the chosen strategy and/ or learning experience address student readiness levels through differentiated instruction?

High Leverage Practices

High leverage practices (HLPs) are instructional and professional practices that enhance or make adjustments to evidence-based instruction (McLeskey et al., 2017). Developed by the Council for Exceptional Children (CEC) and the Collaboration for Effective Educator Development, Accountability and Reform (CEEDAR), these considerations for instructional decision-making focus on four areas: collaboration, assessment, social/emotional/behavioral, and instruction. HLPs provide the intense instructional focus needed to meet the needs of gifted learners (McLeskey & Brownell, 2015) and as such, provide key considerations on how to best implement the chosen strategy into a learning experience to achieve the desired student outcomes. While engaging in coaching conversations focused on HLPs, the GT coach might ask questions such as:

+ How might gifted and high-potential learners grow and develop *interpersonal skills with peers*? (HLP9)
+ How might this strategy provide opportunities to *adapt curriculum tasks and materials* to address gifted and high-potential learners? (HLP13)
+ How might students use *metacognitive thinking* as they learn advanced content? (HLP14)
+ Given the context of your class, what *scaffolded supports* could be integrated to support students in their zone of proximal development? (HLP15)
+ How might *flexible grouping* be integrated within this strategy to best address student readiness levels? (HLP17)
+ How will gifted and high-potential learners feel *actively engaged* in their learning throughout this strategy? (HLP18)
+ In what ways are gifted and high-potential students able to *generalize new learning* through this strategy? (HLP21)

Additional information on HLPs can be found at https://highleveragepractices.org/.

Developing Student Agency

Self-agency is the capacity to take action and shape future outcomes (Bandura, 2006). Phelps and Lewis (2023) note that student agency is centered on how students connect learning to their personal lives, how they find value in the task, and how they accept responsibility to put forth their best effort in achieving that task. The consideration of student agency allows the GT coach and teacher to focus on autonomous learning as a way to increase active student engagement in gifted/high-potential learners. This, in turn, leads to higher achievement and greater self-efficacy (Phelps, 2022). While working through the Blueprint, the GT coach might ask:

+ How will students connect conceptual understandings to their personal life?
+ In knowing students' diverse backgrounds, in what ways might students connect their interests, future goals, and/or identities to new learning?
+ In what ways does this strategy or learning experience provide students with an opportunity to take responsibility and ownership of their learning?

Access Points

The GT coach and teacher should also explore how the selected strategy provides opportunities for gifted/high-potential students to make meaning from the new learning, as well as how "access" provides greater opportunities for equitable gifted identification and talent development. As such, the GT coach and teacher should explore how the strategy and learning experience provide an entry point, or onramp, for students to connect with and make meaning from the content. While focused on this aspect of instructional decision-making, the GT coach might ask questions such as:

+ What previous experience do your students have with the strategy and/or content we have listed? How might this past experience impact how they connect to the new learning associated with your chosen goal?
+ In what ways are students able to make connections between the focused content and their funds of knowledge/life experiences?
+ Given the differentiation needs of your classroom, how might you modify the strategy to provide all students in your classroom to work in their zone of proximal development?
+ In knowing students' current skills and previous exposure to varied instructional strategies, how does this strategy provide entry points to access and engage with advanced content?
+ In analyzing the pre-assessment data of the unit of study, how does the chosen strategy and/or learning experience address student readiness levels through differentiated instruction?

Support the Teacher in Learning the Strategy

Once it is clear how the strategy will be implemented within a specific classroom context, it is now time to support the teacher in feeling confident in implementing the strategy within the classroom. Depending on the teacher's experience level and knowledge of the strategy, itself, the Plan and Act stage of the GT Coaching Circuit might take several different paths at this point:

+ Model the strategy.
+ Co-teach.
+ Co-plan with the teacher.

With the purpose of the goal guiding the plan, each of these options, or a combination of several, provides an opportunity for the teacher to learn more about the strategy and how it might be implemented within their own classroom.

Model the Strategy

There are often times when the teacher is unfamiliar with a particular strategy and would benefit from seeing the strategy "in action." This is often the case for teachers who have not had exposure to professional learning focused on gifted instructional strategies. In these scenarios, it is powerful for the teacher to see the GT coach model the strategy to see it in practice before trying to go "solo." While there are available online videos that demonstrate many popular strategies, it might be beneficial for the teacher to see the strategy within the context of their own classroom. In addition, the reflective coaching session following the modeled session provides an opportunity for the teacher and GT coach to process the shared experience of student outcomes, gifted pedagogy, and instructional planning.

With this being said, remember that GT coaching does not happen *in* the modeling process, itself; it happens in the reflection *before* and *after* the modeling of the strategy. This means that the GT coach and teacher should talk through what the modeled lesson will consist of *before* the actual modeled lesson takes place. As the GT coach, be prepared to share your own thoughts regarding:

+ What considerations were taken into account while planning the modeled lesson?
+ What will guide the instructional decisions throughout the lesson?
+ How are formative assessments integrated throughout the lesson? What scaffolds and opportunities to differentiate "up" are in place if needed?

It is often just as important for the teacher to "hear" the inner dialogue of how the GT coach plans for modeling the lesson as what it is to see it in action.

To provide the teacher with a structure to grow in understanding of the modeled strategy, we created the Observing Instructional Strategies for Gifted Learners (see Resource 5.5; downloadable at www.routledge. com/9781032375144). Some of you might be able to relate to a time when you have modeled a lesson to glance over at a teacher to see papers being graded or emails being read. For any GT coach this would feel discouraging, to say the least. To ensure that the model session is purposeful for both the GT coach and the teacher, Resource 5.5 provides the observing teacher with an objective of citing evidence of practice from the modeled lesson. More specifically, the teacher will be looking for examples of next-level questioning, engagement through accelerated content, integration of depth, complexity, and problem solving, and opportunities for reflective thinking. This resource not only provides a purpose for the teacher in the modeled lesson, it also serves as a third point tool in subsequent coaching conversations. As such, the GT coach could ask guiding questions such as:

+ How did gifted/high-potential students react to the lesson? How might their reactions be similar or different in conjunction with your selected goal? What modifications to the strategy might need to be put in place with these new insights?

+ In what ways did the strategy provide opportunities for students to reveal their talents and demonstrate their strengths? How does this insight align with your goal?

+ What are the next steps in planning to use this strategy as you continue forward in achieving your goal?

Observing Instructional Strategies
for Gifted Learners

Strategies	Evidence in the Lesson
Next Level Questioning + Would you agree or disagree? Why? + What other information do you need? + How could you represent___ with a symbol, phrase, body movement, tableau pose, song title, etc.? + What would be another way to__? + Explain your reasoning. Justify and explain why. + Let's take this a step further . . . what else . . .? + How would ____ see it differently? + What assumptions are made about___?	
Engagement Strategies with Advanced Content + Discuss with a partner or small groups using advanced academic vocabulary. + Act out the concept or process. + Debate the controversy (stand on opposite sides of the room) and construct argument with substantial evidence. + Promote student-student-student talk vs. student-teacher-student.	
Depth, Complexity, Problem-Solving + Big ideas- Relate idea to a universal idea like change, conflict, patterns, systems. + Paradox- How does this show two contrasting ideas? + Parallel- How does this relate to___? + Multiple Perspectives – What are other ways to view___? + Abstract thinking- What metaphor or symbol can we use__? + Connecting Ideas- What factors influence___? What could this lead to? + Change over time- What do you predict? + Problem-Solving around multi-sided problems; multiple solution ideas	

Strategies	Evidence in the Lesson
Reflective Thinking + Opportunities for students' *aha* celebrations or or *uh-oh* clarifications of learning + Relating content to real-world or self + Reflecting on applying methods and thinking of the field/discipline (thinking as a historian, mathematician, etc.) + Cementing the concept through application to real-world contexts	
Teacher Reflection + How did students react to the lesson? + In what ways did the strategies support gifted learners? + What are next steps for instructional planning? + How does this help students make continual progress in their learning?	

Adapted from *Instructional Strategies for Gifted Students Observation* Form by E. Mofield, 2014, Sumner County Schools. Adapted with permission from the author.

Mindfulness in Modeling

As the GT coach proceeds with modeling the strategy, there are additional factors to keep in mind. First and foremost, remember the purpose behind the modeling session. This is an opportunity to build a teacher's capacity through self-reflective practice. For many teachers, this might be the first time they see a particular strategy in action, or it might be the first time they see a strategy targeting the needs of gifted/high-potential learners. Through modeling, GT coaches are often the conduit that leads teachers to self-discovery and professional growth within their own practice. Engage in committed listening to hear their needs and then know how to guide, model, and reflect alongside teachers within the coaching process.

Likewise, GT coaches must also recognize how to structure the modeling session. There are times when it is important to start small and provide the teacher with opportunities to focus on different components of a strategy before diving in too deep. For example, it would not make sense to model all of Kaplan's depth and complexity thinking tools (Kaplan, 2009) at one time. Not only would that be overwhelming, it would also not provide the teacher, or the students, with an opportunity to master the various components for needed success. It would be like jumping into the deep end of the pool without knowing how to tread water. Depending on the experience and knowledge base of the teacher, the GT coach will need to progress with modeling in a manner that is most beneficial in supporting the teacher in achieving their student-focused goal.

Co-teaching

Whether a teacher is still growing in the understanding of a strategy or if they have seen a strategy modeled and still feel as though they need additional support, co-teaching provides a space to co-plan and deliver instruction through co-action. While working to build capacity through GT coaching, Friend and Cook's (2017) Team Teaching provides an opportunity for two teachers to facilitate instruction side by side. In gifted education, we like to think of this as Tango Teaching (Mofield & Phelps, 2020) where the two teachers are directly "in step" with each other as they take turns adding a step, question, or escalated level of challenge to the lesson.

By working side-by-side in this co-teaching model, it should not be evident to the students who the "lead" teacher is, as each teacher is a dynamic member of the instructional team. As such, this provides the GT coach and teacher an invaluable opportunity to support each other during instruction while also providing opportunities to insert personalized nuances. In coaching through co-teaching in this manner, it is often helpful for the teacher to explain the content while the GT coach introduces the learning activity (Knight, 2019). This also provides an opportunity for the teacher to interact with the strategy while knowing that the GT coach is present through this shared experience. Other gifted co-teaching models include Tier Teaching, Carousel Teaching, Scout Teaching, Stretch Teaching, and Safari Teaching (examples in Mofield & Phelps, 2020). Regardless of the co-teaching model, the GT coach and teacher should engage in reflective dialogue following every co-taught class to reflect on progress toward the teacher-selected goal.

Co-Planning with the Teacher

For experienced teachers who are well-versed in the characteristics and learning needs of gifted/high-potential students and/or have a high level of comfort in implementing the chosen strategy, co-planning provides an opportunity for the GT coach and teacher to co-construct a lesson plan together. Through this process, the GT coach can ask foundational questions to further strengthen the plan of action. Questions in co-planning might be modified through the previously mentioned questions focused on HLP's, student agency, and access to focus more intently on how the lesson is incorporating the various considerations of practice. Likewise, in knowing the context of the classroom, the GT coach might lead with more general questions from seeing the foundation of what the teacher is planning. Possible points of dialogue might include:

+ Tell me more about your idea for this part of the lesson.
+ What ideas do you have for co-designing student tasks (e.g., tiered assignments, performance-based tasks)?
+ In what ways might differentiating "up" be integrated at [this point] in the lesson?
+ Given the pre-assessment data, what scaffolds might be put in place to support students in next levels of their learning?

Regardless of whether modeling or co-teaching is used, co-planning is a valuable means for the GT coach and teacher to co-think how to best target the teacher's student-centered goal, and because of this, ongoing reflection is integral to how the coaching conversation evolves.

Reflection as a Common Denominator

Throughout the entire Plan and Act stage, the GT coach and teacher should regularly reflect on the effects of their instructional decision making.

This might involve how modifications to the strategy further challenged gifted/high-potential students or how the selected strategy affected student learning and the desired student outcomes overall. This reflection then opens new co-thinking to explore:

+ In knowing that gifted and high-potential learners were highly engaged through this strategy, in what ways does that inform future instructional decision-making?
+ In what ways were you able to assess that students were working within their zone of proximal development?
+ Given that students mastered the accelerated content quickly, how might you differentiate "up" in the future?

While reflection is a common thread throughout the entire GT Coaching Circuit, reflection will be discussed more intently in Chapter 6.

Set up for Success

By working through the GT Coaching Circuit, the teacher is now developing greater confidence and teacher self-efficacy (i.e., the belief that one's ability can impact student learning). As such, it is now time for the teacher to begin to implement the strategy independently in their own planning and instruction. This is an exciting time, and definitely deserves a celebration! We reiterate that through the steps outlined in this chapter, the GT Coaching Circuit correlates with the ADKAR model for change, specifically in building a teacher's *knowledge* and *ability* related to their established goal.

In some coaching contexts (and depending on the goal selected), the teacher may desire feedback on their use of GT instructional strategies. When the role of a coach is to observe learning and teaching, the role should not be to *evaluate* the teacher, but support the teacher's own construction of new knowledge. The GT coach can center the data collection on the teacher's goal by asking, "What data do you want me to collect in regard to your goal?" From here, the GT coach focuses on collecting evidence related to this aim. This data might be related to the teacher's actions (e.g., asks high-level questions, creates opportunities for transfer, builds off student responses to differentiate "up") and student learning (e.g., creates generalizations, thinks as a disciplinarian, makes connections upon multiple ideas, demonstrates intense focus). After collecting the data, the GT coach can support the teacher in making subsequent conclusions.

For example, if a teacher desires for the coach to collect data on how students use critical thinking (as this relates to the teacher's goal), the GT coach may note that students were engaged in student-to-student interactions in response to a debatable question. They built arguments with logical evidence while considering points of view and assumptions (using elements of reasoning), using a graphic organizer to plan their thinking.

The reflective dialogue around this evidence may allow for the GT coach and teacher to discuss how aspects of the ABC's of Differentiation are related to the data collected. The GT coach might ask:

+ What does the data reveal about student learning?
+ What connections can you make between your actions/decisions and your students' thinking?
+ How do the ABCs of Differentiation relate to your actions and student outcomes?

The teacher can identify patterns and connections between their instructional decisions and student learning. As these connections are uncovered, the teacher is able to create meaning, seeing firsthand the impact of their own actions. For example, the teacher might conclude that by intentionally posing a forced-choice question to students with a specific model (e.g., Paul's reasoning), this led to an opportunity for students to use critical thinking and examine diverse perspectives. As a teacher reflects on these patterns during the coaching dialogue, they grow in their confidence and capacity to challenge gifted and high-potential students.

Resource 5.6 (downloadable at www.routledge.com/9781032375144) is an example of a data collection form that can be used to facilitate reflection. After the data collection is complete, the GT coach can offer the data to the teacher and ask the teacher to make conclusions (using the reflection questions to guide the conversation as needed). The ABCs of Differentiation are included so that the teacher can reflect on how the collected data links to gifted-related pedagogy. We emphasize that the ABCs are *not* a checklist for observing components in the lesson. The ABCs are included only to provide an opportunity to discuss how student thinking is facilitated by these features.

Take time to reflect on how each of the steps within the GT Coaching Circuit provide you with an opportunity to look forward. This will be a key factor in the final phase of the GT Coaching Circuit.

Data Collection Form: Student Learning and Teacher Actions

Teacher's Goal

Data Collected
Student interactions, engagement, questions, outcomes, etc.
Teacher actions, questions, use of materials, etc.

Reflection
+ What does the data reveal about student learning?
+ What connections can you make between your actions/decisions and your students' thinking?
+ How do the ABC's of Differentiation relate to your actions and student outcomes?

ABC's of Differentiation

Advance the Content	Build the Buy-In	Create Challenge	Determine Scaffolds
+ Accelerate content + Advanced resources + Advanced vocabulary + Content-expert thinking + Above grade level standards	+ Choices + Agency + Funds of Knowledge + Real-world connection + Create task value tied to identity, interest, future	+ Open inquiry + Depth/complexity + Creative thinking + Critical thinking + High-level thinking + Abstract thinking + Critical thinking + Transfer + Metacognition	+ Sentence stems + Graphic organizers + Visual Aids + Prompts + Checklists + Chunking

Summary

The second stage of the GT Coaching Circuit, Plan and Act, incorporates the ADKAR model of change by building the teacher's gifted pedagogical "knowledge" and "ability" to grow in differentiated instructional practice. Within this stage, the GT coach and teacher choose a strategy or model and learn how to use the strategy considering the what, why, and how as it is related to the needs of gifted and high-potential learners. Teachers are supported in learning the strategy through modeling, co-teaching, and/or co-planning, and once the teacher is ready, they independently use the strategy within their own planning and instruction. The GT Toolkit of Strategies and Thinking Models (see Appendix C) serves as a powerful reference throughout this stage of the GT Coaching Circuit.

Reflection Questions

1. How does knowing the context of the classroom in conjunction with the teacher-selected goal impact the "Plan and Act" stage of the GT Coaching Circuit?
2. How do High Leverage Practices (HLPs) provide additional considerations for differentiation for supporting gifted and high-potential students in their learning?
3. How do the structures provided in the Plan and Act stage align with the elements of SCARF (i.e., status, certainty, autonomy, relatedness, and fairness)?
4. Review Appendix C and D. What other strategies and models might you add to these lists? Then, choose a strategy and complete your own Tool Template to familiarize yourself with its use.

Coaching Notes: Plan and Act

SUPPORT MATERIAL

Plan and Act	Coaching Notes	Coaching Prompts
Select and Learn a Strategy		+ *What do you want to focus on?*
		+ *You value_____. It's exciting to see_____.*
Select a Strategy		+ *What would happen if_____?*
–Choose a strategy to implement, considering its purpose and impact on student outcomes.		+ *I'm curious about that . . . .*
+ *How does the desired student outcome align with the purpose of the strategy?*		+ *Tell me more . . .*
+ *How does the strategy engage gifted and high-potential students as a means to increase academic achievement and student growth?*		+ *So, in other words_____? Is that right?*
		+ *So, you are saying_____.*
+ *How does the strategy provide opportunities for students to make connections, problem-solve, or accelerate their learning?*		
+ *Use the Tool Template: What, Why, How*		
–Elicit teacher input with GT Instructional Blueprint:		
+ *How do you think you might modify this with your students?*		
Support the Teacher in Learning the Strategy		
–Discuss options for co-action:		
+ Model the strategy (bite-sized modeling).		
+ Co-teach the strategy through a shared vision.		
+ Co-plan a lesson with the teacher.		
Set up for Success		
–When the teacher is ready, the teacher uses the strategy in own planning and instruction.		
–Provide reflective feedback on use of strategy (if requested).		

References

Bandura, A. (2006). Toward a psychology of human agency. Perspectives on Psychological Science, 1, 164–180.

Cohen, J. (1988). *Statistical power analysis for the behavioral sciences* (2nd ed.). Lawrence Erlbaum Associates, Publishers.

de Bono, E. (2016). *Six thinking hats.* Penguin. (Original work published 1985)

Fisher, D., Frey, N., & Hattie, J. (2016). *Visible learning for literacy, grades K–12 : Implementing the practices that work best to accelerate student learning.* Corwin.

Friend, M., & Cook, L. (2017). *Interactions: Collaboration skills for professionals* (8th ed.). Allyn & Bacon.

Guilford, J. P. (1986). *Creative talents: Their nature, uses and development.* Bearly.

Hattie, J. (2012). *Visible learning for teachers.* Routledge.

Hattie, J. (2017). Visible learning MetaX. https://www.visiblelearningmetax.com/Influences.

Hiatt, J.M. (2006). *ADKAR: A model for change in business, government and our community.* Prosci Research.

Holland, D.C., Lachicotte, W., Skinner, D., & Cain, C. (1998). *Identity and agency in cultural worlds.* Harvard University Press.

Johnston, P.H. (2004). *Choice words: How our language affects children's learning.* Stenhouse Publishers.

Kaplan, S. (2009). Layering differentiated curricula for the gifted and talented. In F. A. Karnes & S. M. Bean (Eds.), *Methods and materials for teaching the gifted* (3rd ed., pp. 107–156). Prufrock Press.

Knight, J. (2019). Instructional coaching for implementing visible learning: A model for translating research into practice. *Educational Sciences, 9*(101), 1–16. https://doi.org/10.3390/educsci9020101.

McLeskey, J., Barringer, M-D., Billingsley, B., Brownell, M., Jackson, D., Kennedy, M., Lewis, T., Maheady, L., Rodriguez, J., Scheeler, M. C., Winn, J., & Ziegler, D. (2017, January). *High-leverage practices in special education.* Council for Exceptional Children & CEEDAR Center.

McLeskey, J., & Brownell, M. (2015). *High-leverage practices and teacher preparation in special education* (Document No. PR-1). Retrieved from University of Florida, Collaboration for Effective Educator, Development, Accountability, and Reform Center website: http://ceedar.education.ufl.edu/wp-content/uploads/2015/10/Practice-Review-Mcleskey-Brownell.pdf.

Mofield, E. (2023). *Vertical differentiation for gifted, advanced, and high-potential students: 25 strategies to stretch student thinking.* Routledge Press.

Mofield, E., & Phelps, V. (2020). *Collaboration, coteaching, and coaching in gifted education: Sharing strategies to support gifted learners.* Prufrock Press.

Phelps, V. (2022). Motivating gifted adolescents through the power of PIE: Preparedness, innovation, and effort. *Roeper Review, 44*(1), 35–48. https://doi.10.1080/02783193.2021.2005204.

Phelps, V., & Lewis, K. (2023). *Strength-based goal setting in gifted education: Addressing social emotional awareness, self-advocacy, and underachievement in gifted education.* Routledge Press.

Toshalis, E. (2015). *Make me! Understanding and engaging student resistance in school.* Harvard Education Press.

Vygotsky, L. S. (1978). *Mind in society: The development of higher psychological processes.* Harvard University Press.

Chapter 6

The Coaching Circuit

Reflect

While reflective practice is a consistent thread throughout GT coaching, the third stage of the GT Coaching Circuit provides the dedicated time and space for the coach and teacher to intently reflect on the relationship between instructional practice and student outcomes. It gives permission to hit the pause button and re-examine how gifted and high-potential students' learning needs are addressed through the selected strategy. This reflective process also provides the opportunity to explore next steps for moving forward. By engaging in these coaching conversations, teachers can reflect upon and recognize how their instructional decision-making impacts the desired student outcomes. This stage of the coaching circuit includes the following:

+ Reflect on the established goal.
+ Reflect on the process of the teacher's growth.
+ Reflecting on next steps.

Essentially, this stage allows teachers to reflect "Where are students now? How did they get here? How did my actions influence this? Where do we go next?" At the end of this chapter, we have provided Resource 6.1: Reflect- Coaching Notes to guide and support teachers through the third stage of the GT Coaching Circuit. In addition, Appendix B provides an example of a coaching conversation that represents how a GT coach and classroom teacher navigate each stage of the coaching circuit.

DOI: 10.4324/9781003340560-7

Reflect on Goal Attainment

The reflection process begins with identifying the desired student outcomes and examining evidence. The GT coach might ask, "What was the goal? To what extent did students achieve it? How do we know?" With this information, the GT coach and teacher are prepared to examine collected data.

Revisit Goal

First, bring attention to the goal established in Stage 1. What did the teacher want the students to think and do? What was the criteria for success? As the GT coach, you may have written the teacher-established goal down in the coaching notes. This goal may have focused on students achieving above grade level standards, applying higher levels of critical thinking into learning tasks, or using more advanced problem solving. As the goal is discussed, be sure to anchor the conversation in possibility rather than *should have* statements that focus on the past. For example, if the coaching discussion focuses on *should haves* (i.e., "I should have done more for my gifted/high potential students," "I should have paid more attention at that gifted training," or "I should have pre-assessed to learn my students' readiness levels"), this robs the opportunity of moving forward through reflection in a proactive manner. Instead, dialogue around the goal should drive next steps (e.g., "Where do we go from here?").

Clearly communicate that goals do not have a one-size-fits-all time frame in which they need to be achieved. Take the time to normalize that many goals take time and remain cognizant that reflection *on* action and reflection *for* action are both needed (Schon, 1983). While some goals might be achieved early, other goals might take weeks, months, or even longer, depending on the goal, the classroom context, and the available resources. The key is to recognize and celebrate the small successes along the way.

Reflect on Evidence

Once the desired student outcomes are at the forefront of the coaching conversation, the GT coach engages the teacher in reflecting on current levels of student progress in relation to the goal. Initial questions might be more general in nature to "prime the pump" before progressing into deeper reflections focused on evidence of practice and data assessment. These first reflective questions might consist simply of "What has gone well?" or "What has surprised you in moving through this process?" Because reflective practice often requires such vulnerability, these early questions also provide the space to re-establish the aspects of the TEAM framework (i.e., Trust, Engage, Align, Maintain).

Here it is important to revisit the criteria established in Stage 1 when the coach asked, "What might the goal look like? What are the criteria for success?" As the reflective conversation progresses to evidence of practice, the questions become more specific in nature. The teacher begins to recognize how gifted/high-potential learners' needs were addressed, as well as how all students were given opportunities to develop their talents. The goal is to create the *aha* moments for the collaborating teacher to recognize how addressing the readiness levels for gifted/high-potential learners also sets the context for addressing the readiness levels for typical learners. In turn, all students have greater opportunities for success.

In discussing how the teacher knows the goal is achieved, it is important to specify this evidence. For example, if a teacher shares that progress was made because students "seemed" more engaged in their learning, then the GT coach could follow with questions to guide the teacher into evaluating *how* the levels of engagement might be measured. This evidence could be either quantitative (e.g., assessment scores, time on task, percentage of work completion) or qualitative (e.g., positive insights shared on reflections, intense focus on learning tasks, meaningful connections).

Table 6.1 provides examples of both quantitative and qualitative evidence for measuring progress toward student-focused outcomes. Remember that each goal might have different types of evidence to signify student progress. For example, you might refer to evidence for how students showed critical and creative thinking in their assignments or tasks (refer to Resource 5.2 Critical Thinking and Creative Thinking Considerations for Strategy Selection, Chapter 5). Additionally, if the teacher wanted you to directly collect evidence of their teaching, together you may discuss data collected from Resource 5.6. Data Collection: Student Learning and Teacher Action form (see Chapter 5).

TABLE 6.1

Quantitative and Qualitative Evidence for Student-Focused Outcomes

Examples of Quantitative Evidence	Examples of Qualitative Evidence
+ Summative assessment scores + Formative assessment scores + Actual time on task + Percentage of work completion + Survey/Likert Scale scores	+ Personal insights shared on reflections + Intense focus on learning task + Personalized and/or meaningful connections to learning + Participation in class discussions + Affective traits (e.g., smiling, excitement, perseverance)

The Reflect-Coaching Notes (see Resource 6.1) provides a space to record and process the coaching conversation with the teacher. A few examples of questions to ask about the data include the following:

+ What evidence are you seeing that signifies the chosen strategy is being successful?
+ What progress has been made in relation to the desired student outcomes? How do you know?
+ How did the selected strategy impact gifted and high-potential students?
+ How did this strategy impact other students?
+ How did the strategy allow opportunities to reveal talent and recognize student strengths?
+ In what ways did students demonstrate critical thinking?
+ In what ways did students show creative thinking?
+ In what ways were students challenged to be flexible in their thinking?
+ In what ways were students able to make connections and create generalizations?
+ In what ways were students able to think as a subject matter expert?
+ What, if any, barriers or roadblocks did you encounter? How did you navigate them?
+ What are students' next steps in learning?

We cannot stress enough the importance of recording the shared, reflective thoughts of the teacher on the coaching notes (see Resource 6.1). This is needed for several reasons. First, recording this evidence provides an opportunity to engage in coaching conversations that are focused on an explicit, shared understanding. By making the reflective thoughts visible on the coaching notes, the thinking becomes more concrete. In doing so, the reflective thoughts begin to articulate a greater vision of how gifted/high-potential students are working toward the desired outcome, as well as spotting talent in those who might not have yet been identified.

In addition, insights and evidence recorded on the coaching notes serve as a portfolio of sorts for the GT coach and teacher. As previously discussed, GT coaching is not a "one and done" endeavor. It is individualized professional learning for the teacher that builds capacity and creates lasting change over time. As with anything worth learning, change does not happen overnight. As the GT coach and teacher engage in coaching conversations over time, these notes and evidence of practice serve as a window to deeper reflection. The recorded information allows the GT coach and teacher to celebrate progress over time, recognize trends in student learning, and develop a greater awareness for how instructional practices impact talent development.

Reflect on Building Capacity

GT coaching is founded on building capacity in teachers' instructional practice. As such, the GT coach now engages the teacher in deeper levels of metacognition. The goal is for the teacher to develop an awareness of how instructional decision-making is connected to student outcomes. Once these connections are made, the teacher begins to explore more intently how their instructional decision-making is further influenced through core beliefs and culturally responsive teaching practices. The GT coach provides the space for the teacher to recognize and celebrate their own development of self-efficacy (e.g., how well a person believes they will be able to reach a desired outcome in a given context; Bandura, 1997). In doing so, the GT coach is seeking to answer the following questions:

+ How is the teacher able to gain awareness in recognizing the impact on student outcomes based on instructional decision-making?
+ What considerations of instructional design might lead the teacher to make sustainable changes of practice across varying instructional contexts?

Reflecting on the process of the teacher's growth is another dynamic dimension of GT coaching.

Make Connections between Student Outcomes and Instructional Decisions

The GT coach is now able to guide the teacher in making connections between instructional decisions and the resulting student outcomes. This strengthens teacher efficacy. Figure 6.1 illustrates the RISE Teacher Efficacy Model. Through this model, the GT coach and teacher enter the coaching conversation through a reflective mindset that focuses on the teacher identifying key instructional decisions. The teacher is then guided to make connections between the instructional decisions/actions and the resulting student responses/outcomes. As the teacher continues in this manner, the teacher's reflective mindset continues to "rise" to a greater level of awareness and efficacy. Key considerations of practice regarding the classroom context, ABC's of Differentiation, student agency, access points, high leverage practices, and talent development are provided as references for the GT coach to guide the teacher in this process.

FIGURE 6.1
RISE Teacher Efficacy Model

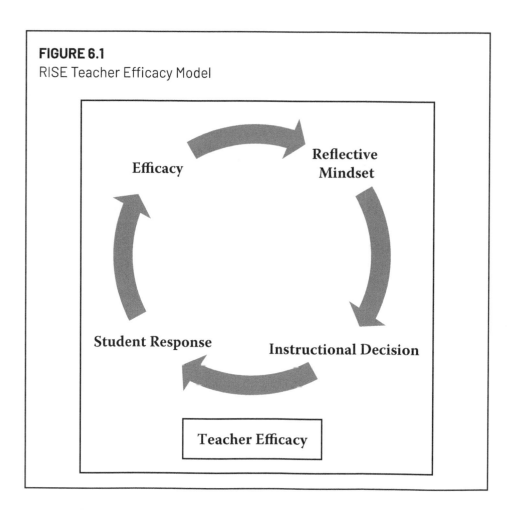

As you engage with a teacher through the RISE model, you might guide the teacher by asking questions such as:

+ When you did this _____what did you notice from your students?
+ Identify a key instructional decision in your lesson. How did gifted and high-potential learners react? How did other students react?
+ What instructional decisions do you believe made the greatest impact on gifted and high potential learner outcomes?
+ Which student behaviors informed how you would adapt your instruction? Were those adaptations successful? Why/Why not?
+ Were there any moments when you felt insecure in your instructional decisions during a particular lesson? What was the basis of that insecurity?
+ Were there any moments when you felt particularly strong in your instructional decision-making during a particular lesson? What was the basis of that confidence?

+ Did you find that you were making more/less adaptations for students at any particular readiness level?

+ What action(s) from you elicited greater student engagement from gifted and high-potential learners? How did this manifest in your students and what were the resulting effects?

+ Was there any instructional decision that you had not planned for? What were the factors that led to that decision, and what were the resulting student outcomes?

Make Connections between Core Beliefs and Instructional Decisions

As the GT coach and teacher reflect on how instructional decisions impact student learning, there is an additional opportunity to delve deeper into strengthening the teacher's metacognition by reflecting on how a teacher's core beliefs impact instruction. The GT coach might begin by asking, "How have you grown in your own awareness of the needs of gifted and high-potential learners?" The following questions provide additional opportunities to engage in reflective dialogue that is more specifically geared toward a teacher's core beliefs and their impact on instructional decision-making as related to the student-focused goal.

+ In thinking about your instructional decision-making, how are your core beliefs regarding how gifted/high-potential students learn evident?

+ In reflecting on your instructional decision making, are there any assumptions about gifted/ high-potential learners that potentially impact your instructional practice? If so, in what way?

+ How do your core beliefs about student learning impact the role of student agency within your classroom?

+ How might the core beliefs you have about your own learning impact the instructional decisions within your classroom?

Core Values Applied to Culturally Responsive Teaching

As the teacher's self-awareness of core values and instructional decision-making become more explicit, the GT coach should guide the teacher to recognize how core beliefs also relate to specific considerations such as equitable access to talent development. The GT coach might ask the following questions to guide the teacher in this process:

+ In valuing positive student outcomes, how might students' different backgrounds have impacted their ability to demonstrate their level of understanding on advanced content (positively or negatively)? What other adjustments could be made?

+ In what ways were student outcomes directly affected by modifications made to provide greater access in learning? How does this connect to your core beliefs about how gifted and high-potential students learn?

+ How was your instructional decision-making impacted by recognizing and respecting students' different perspectives to learning? How do these different perspectives enhance transfer of knowledge?

+ In what ways does this metacognitive reflection provide insight to better meet the learning needs of gifted and high-potential learners?

Reflect Forward

Reflecting is not just about looking back, it is also looking forward. As previously stated, it is never meant to anchor us in the *should have* past; reflection propels us to forward action. The ultimate objective of coaching is to drive change and growth so the teacher can apply what has been learned to future instructional practice. Reflecting forward is a time to celebrate, transfer learning to new contexts, and plan next steps.

Celebrate

As the GT coach and teacher examine the evidence of student learning, it will either be determined that the goal has been met, or to the contrary, it has not. Each scenario has its own celebrations. First, for the goal that has been met, make sure to celebrate the accomplishment, and reflect on what steps led to successful goal attainment. In what ways did the coaching process support the teacher in the process? In what ways was the teacher able to build self-efficacy through the process? In what ways was the GT coach able to grow and evolve in their understanding of gifted and high-potential learners? Celebrate the co-thinking and co-action that led to this point, and use that celebration to begin to identify a new goal with the teacher.

Transfer

The GT coach should also guide the teacher in recognizing how this success transfers to other contexts. The GT coaching process is meant to create capacity that leads to sustainable change. While this is a process that happens over time, the GT coach and teacher should explore how the lessons learned through the coaching experience might apply across different contexts (e.g., content area, grade level). For the GT coach, this outcome is the icing on the cake. You might ask:

+ How might this strategy be used in other content areas?
+ How might this strategy be used with a different group of students?
+ In what ways might this strategy be used in an upcoming unit?
+ How might you co-plan with a colleague for an interdisciplinary unit using this strategy?

Revise Goal

It is possible, as well, that the desired student outcomes were not achieved. While some might view this as a detriment, it is actually a powerful moment in refining instructional practice. This, also, is a celebration. At this time, the GT coach and teacher have both learned more about what has worked well and which areas might need extra attention. In these cases, the GT coach and teacher can reference the coaching notes and additional data to inform next steps on how to refine the goal. They can reflect on what worked well and move forward with that in mind. During these coaching conversations, remain focused on the reflective insights gained on stretching gifted and high-potential students in their learning. In determining next steps, the GT coach might ask:

+ What are the future desired student outcomes? Do the outcomes need any modifications, or does the chosen strategy need to be refined/readdressed?
+ What current evidence and insights do we have regarding the goal? In what ways does this information provide direction to refining future instructional practice in working toward the goal?
+ In understanding past practice and students' backgrounds, how might instructional practice be refined to achieve the desired student outcomes?

During this reflection, the teacher might share that the selected strategy did not stretch the students to engage in critical thinking to the degree that was desired. Through the ongoing coaching conversations, the GT coach and teacher examine if students did not reach the desired outcome due to limitations of the strategy, lack of core foundational knowledge, lack of student buy-in with the strategy, or other factors that might be identified. With this information, the GT coach and teacher can determine 1.) if a strategy needs to be modified based on student need, 2.) if a different strategy might need to be explored, 3) if the goal needs to be modified (e.g., criteria), or 4.), or if no adaptations are needed. It might also be determined that students just need more time with the strategy. This is also an opportunity to refer back to the GT Blueprint (Resource 5.4) to re-examine how additional high-leverage practices, access points, and student agency might lead to greater success in meeting the needs of gifted and high-potential learners.

Depending on the determined course of action, the GT coach and teacher can move forward with making the appropriate revisions. As the GT coach and teacher work through this process, the collaborative team might decide on additional opportunities for co-planning, co-teaching, modeling, and/or observing other teachers.

Plan Next Steps

Reflection is one part of the GT coaching process that occurs over time and provides opportunities to revisit a teacher-selected goal. It also reflects the final stage of the ADKAR model (Hiatt, 2006), reinforcement. Reflection as a form of "reinforcement" supports the ability to build capacity and grow teacher-efficacy in addressing the needs of gifted and high-potential learners.

Remember that coaching is an ongoing process. As such, each coaching session should end with forward thinking. This not only helps to maintain the coaching relationship, it also continues to signify the perpetual thinking associated with consistent growth and co-thinking focused on meeting the needs of gifted/high-potential students. As the GT coach guides the teacher in forward thinking and next steps, questions might consist of:

+ When should we plan on meeting again?
+ What tasks and/or responsibilities should be completed prior to our next meeting?
+ When should those tasks and/or responsibilities be completed by? (Set dates.)
+ How are you prioritizing your next steps in working toward goal attainment?
+ On a scale of 1 to 5, how committed are you to achieving this goal?
+ How will your commitment be evident?

Summary

Overall, this chapter recognizes the role of reflection as a means to develop "reinforcement" of new learning through the ADKAR change model. Within this stage, the GT coach and teacher first revisit the goal to provide purposeful reflection on the extent to which the goal was achieved. Specific attention is given to reflecting on how gifted and high-potential students were impacted through instructional decision-making and lesson design. One of the most powerful components of this stage stems from teachers engaging in deeper levels of metacognition focused on their own personal growth in gifted pedagogy and teacher efficacy. Through forward reflection, the GT coach and teacher celebrate lessons learned, reflect upon transfer of learning to new contexts, and identify the next steps of GT coaching by creating a new goal or revising an existing one.

Reflection Questions

1. How does reflection impact the GT coaching cycle? In what ways does it encourage teacher-efficacy?
2. In what ways is a teacher's metacognition impacted by their understanding of gifted and high potential learners? How might this impact "in-the-moment" instructional decision-making?
3. How does the Reflect stage of the coaching circuit leverage the elements of TEAM (i.e., Trust, Engage, Align, Maintain)?
4. Read through Appendix B: Coaching Scenario. As you read through the coaching conversation, what aspect of reflective dialogue do you see present through all three stages of the coaching circuit? In what ways is the reflective dialogue in the third stage *different* than during "Set a Purpose" and "Plan and Act"?

Coaching Notes: Reflect

Reflect	Coaching Notes	Coaching Prompts
Reflect on student learning and next steps		+ *What do you want to focus on?* + *You value_____. It's exciting to see_____.* + *Would happen if_____?* + *I'm curious about that . . . .* + *Tell me more . . .* + *So, in other words_____? Is that right?* + *So, you are saying_____.*
Reflect on Goal Attainment -Revisit the Goal + *What was the goal? To what extent did students achieve it?* -Reflect on Evidence + *How did the selected strategy impact gifted and high-potential students? Other students? Reveal talent and recognize student strengths?* + *In what ways did you observe students showing creative thinking? Critical thinking? Making connections?, etc.* **Reflect on Building Capacity** -Make connections between student outcomes and teacher decisions + *When you did this_____, what did you notice from students?* **Reflect Forward** -Celebrate -Transfer to new contexts + *How might this strategy be used in other content areas? with a different group of students?in an upcoming unit?* -Revise Goal/Plan Next Steps + *What are your next steps?* + *Do you want to revise the goal?* + *When can we meet again?*		

SUPPORT MATERIAL

References

Bandura, A. (1997). *Self-efficacy: The exercise of control.* W. H. Freeman/Times Books/ Henry Holt & Co.

Hiatt, J.M. (2006). *ADKAR: A model for change in business, government and our community.* Prosci Research.

Schon, D. (1983). *The reflective practitioner.* Basic Books.

Chapter 7

Building Collective Capacity for Change

In this chapter, we go beyond describing the granular pieces of the GT Coaching Circuit and move to explaining the foundational structures for supporting GT coaching from a systems lens. This requires considering existing structures that are in place and the extent to which they facilitate or hinder the collaborative work of coaching. We share how to make a plan for GT coaching visible, defensible, and sustainable by developing a shared vision with administrators. We discuss the importance of aligning aims with other school-based goals, leveraging collective efficacy, working with PLCs or other school-based teams, and using GT coaching as a means towards promoting equity in identifying and serving students from underrepresented groups.

Aligning Vision with Administrators

As we have emphasized throughout this book, Certainty (i.e., C in SCARF) and Maintain (i.e., M in TEAM) are important components to any collaborative relationship, including your relationship with the administration. As you begin your work as a GT coach, it is important to work with the administrators of the school to establish clarity around your role. Your role cannot be supported unless it is understood.

DOI: 10.4324/9781003340560-8

You might consider sharing your job description (we provide suggestions in Chapter 2), the vision of GT coaching as proposed by the Gifted Services Department, and/or your own personal coaching vision. You can also ask administrators their vision of GT coaching. This allows for alignment (i.e., "A" in TEAM) of expectations about the role of the GT coach. You could provide the definition of a GT coach (or modify for your own context) and summarize your areas of focus in three or four major bullet points so the administrator clearly understands your purpose. For example, the GT coach builds capacity in teachers to:

+ Maximize access to rigor for all students.
+ Differentiate "up" by providing additional challenge to high-potential/ gifted students.
+ Identify high-potential students from underrepresented groups.

Refer to Chapter 2 for more specific ideas regarding how GT coaches support teachers.

Perhaps serving as a GT coach is a new endeavor for you. In some contexts, GT coaches also provide direct services to gifted students such as teaching in a pull-out setting. With the administrator, consider addressing these questions:

+ How will your expanded role be communicated to other teachers in the school?
+ How will they perceive that you are not doing separate work with students but that you are a resource supporting teachers to address the needs of gifted students all day, every day?

Discuss with your administrator that your work is not siloed work. As we have previously shared in Chapter 2, GT coaching is integrally linked to goals of the district, the goals of the GT program, and school-wide improvement goals. We show Figure 7.1 again (this was also in Chapter 1, Figure 1.2) to emphasize that the GT coaching is part of a larger system that moves the cogs forward to ultimately influence student learning. All change is complex. One individual cannot change a system overnight. As the GT coach, you are one part (a very key part) of a larger system of pieces that move together to facilitate the overall vision to identify, serve, and challenge gifted and high-potential students.

Connected Planning Guide

A plan is needed to show how the school, district, and GT program are integrated and connected to the role of the GT coach, administrator, and classroom teacher. Resource 7.1- The Connected Planning Guide provides a structure for discussing how the administrator will support the efforts of the GT

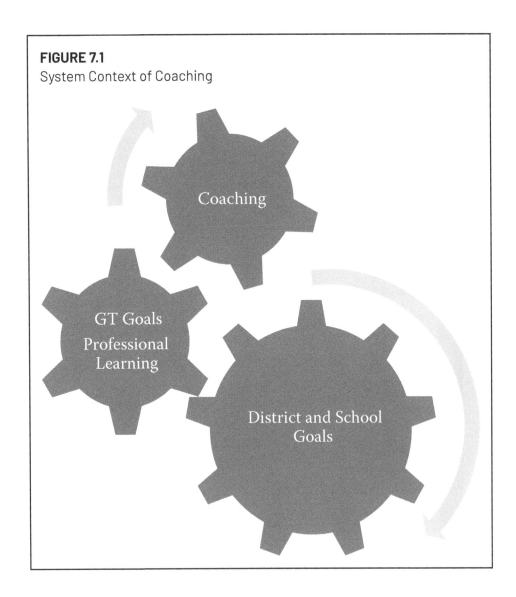

FIGURE 7.1
System Context of Coaching

coach, how the GT coach facilitates the goals of the school/district and GT program, and how the role of the classroom teacher fits within the plan. This provides an opportunity for the administrator and the GT coach to commit to a shared set of goals to guide action. If there is no visible plan or goal, then there are no opportunities to evaluate progress. Structure promotes function. The structure of the Connected Planning Guide promotes the sustainable work of GT coaching.

The Connected Planning Guide

Goals (school and district level)	Roles and Resources from Each Individual			Criteria for Success
	G/T Teacher	Administrator	Roles of Regular Education Teachers	
School-Improvement Plan Goal				
District Strategic Gifted Goal				
District-Wide Goal				

How does the GT Office Strategic Plan connect to the district plan? To the school plan?

How will the school support professional learning to achieve these goals?

Suppose a school improvement plan goal is to maximize access to high-level learning for all students. The GT coach has an opportunity to discuss what this means for gifted and high-potential students. Moreover, if the GT program's goal is to increase equitable identification of gifted students from underserved populations by 5%, a dialogue can take place about specific actions the GT coach, administrator, and classroom teachers will take for this to become a reality. If a district goal is to provide robust instruction in the regular education classroom according to student readiness, specific details can be outlined for students who have advanced readiness levels.

The Connected Planning Guide makes invisible assumptions visible, serving as a communication tool to convey where you are, where you are going, and how you can be supported. Essentially, an administrator must see the plan in order to support the plan. In following, this sets the stage for linking the plan to a larger set of school-based goals and plays a role in contributing to teachers' collective efficacy where all teachers see their role in impacting student learning among *all* students.

Additionally, the Connected Planning Guide may serve as a launching point for planning professional learning based on the school's need. This may be a prime opportunity to work as a team with teachers and administrators on planning professional learning tailored to the goals outlined from the guide. In many instances, the GT coach may lead these professional learning sessions, speak regularly at faculty meetings, or work with grade-level teams to bring action to the plan.

Setting Expectations

An initial conversation is also an opportunity to discuss expectations for GT coaching at your school. In some schools, administrators set an expectation that every teacher meets with the coach once or twice per semester. In some schools, perhaps every "cluster" teacher is expected to work with the coach. Discuss if this is an appropriate approach for your context. Keep in mind that buy-in is more likely to occur when teachers volunteer to participate in coaching. As the saying goes, "what we insist, they will resist." If GT coaching is a new endeavor at your school, consider focusing on working only with volunteer teachers at the start. Another option is to begin coaching a group of teachers rather than individual teachers. We describe this later in this chapter.

As you converse about how the administration might support your role, discuss scheduling issues such as cluster grouping gifted students (i.e., intentionally grouping six to eight gifted students in a classroom so that differentiation is more manageable). This would allow the GT coach to focus efforts on coaching teachers who teach in classrooms with clustered gifted students rather than spreading themselves thin to coach all teachers.

This conversation might also include a discussion about time to collaborate. How will time be allocated for coaching and other forms of collaboration? Some schools have found success with hiring a rotating substitute so that the coach can have time to conduct 30-minute conferences with teachers. Time is indeed a luxury. We must be clear, however, that GT coaching will not be effective or sustainable if there is no time for coaching to happen.

Because your GT role expands beyond focusing only on identified gifted students, this may be a new idea to teachers and even the administration. If one of the goals of GT coaching is to maximize access to rigor for all students, this shift must be communicated thoughtfully and intentionally to teachers. How will it be conveyed to teachers that through a talent development lens, your collaborative coaching also enhances opportunities to provide challenging contexts to not only cultivate talent, but *reveal* it, even among students who are not formally identified as gifted?

In an initial meeting, you may determine how you will communicate with the administration and how often. You might also discuss priorities for how your coaching kicks off. How and when will you be introduced to the faculty? Will you meet first with individuals as volunteers? With grade level teams? Are there specific topics that need to be addressed to the entire faculty in professional learning?

You might also find that classroom teachers could feel uneasy about establishing high expectations for rigor among all students. You might hear, "My students could never do that. They are not ready for this." In your conversations with the administrator, you may need to discuss the perceptions of high expectations among teachers in the school. Is rigor simply a buzzword, or is it executed in daily instructional practice? Do students show evidence of deep learning in their work? What are teachers' beliefs about differentiation? Addressing these concerns with the administration can be a way to align your own expectations with the school climate and culture.

Visible Vertical Differentiation

What might the administrator expect to see in classrooms as a result of GT coaching? How does the work of coaching translate into day-to-day teaching practices? You may share a checklist much like what is shown on Resource 7.2. This shows a number of "look-fors" in classroom instruction. This resource is based on the ABCs of Vertical Differentiation (differentiating "up") (Mofield, 2023) as a guide to provide instruction for gifted/high-potential students. This does not serve as an evaluation form, but as a quick tool for an administrator to use in walk-throughs or other informal observations. Please note that it would not be expected for every box to be checked. The components on this checklist only serve to provide guidance on what vertical differentiation looks like in the classroom. Other aspects of quality teaching (e.g., evidence of student engagement, use of assessments) can be viewed through these features.

ABC Checklist for Vertical Differentiation

Advance the Content	Present	Evidence
- Use of advanced resources		
- Accelerated/flexible pace		
- Use of above-grade level standards		
- Student groupings based on readiness levels		
- Thinks as an "expert" within the discipline		
Build the Buy-In		
- Tasks tied to student interest		
- Tasks incorporate student backgrounds/culture		
- Student-choice is incorporated through lesson		
- Students connect learning to future/real-world application		
- Students have opportunities to develop authentic products		
Create the Challenge		
Open inquiry		
- Explore issues or problems with few parameters		
- Engaged in problem-based learning		
Depth		
- Justify a conclusion about an issue		
- Examine evidence, trends, and patterns of a discipline		
Complexity		
- Make connections among multiple ideas		
- Explore multiple perspectives		
- Examine multiple elements and their interactions		
Critical Thinking		
- Analyze, evaluate, and construct arguments		
- Examine missing parts		
- Make judgments		
- Question arguments		
- Judge credibility and evidence		
- Examine how parts work together as a whole		
- Defend a hypothesis		

Creative Thinking - Develop alternative solutions - Make connections between two seemingly unrelated things - Redesign or rearrange for a specific purpose - Develop a new approach or plan - Synthesize ideas		
Transfer - Extend learning to apply to other disciplines - Apply learning to real-world contexts - Create generalizations and connect to other contexts		
Metacognition - Reflect on their own thinking, identifying challenges and problem-solving approaches - Reflect on next steps in their learning - Reflect on their own development of strengths/talent		

Adapted from Mofield (2023).

How Do We Get Buy-In?

We are often asked, "How do we create teacher buy-in to participate in coaching?" or sometimes, "How can I convince others that what I am asking them to do (i.e., engage in the coaching process) is important and impactful?"

When we were both working as a consulting teachers for gifted education (in somewhat of a coaching role) for a school district, we remember feeling as if we were trying to "sell" something, like girl-scout cookies, with high hopes that we could collaboratively partner with teachers. Over time, we realized it was not about us presenting a persuasive argument with justifiable evidence for why and how differentiation would challenge gifted students. The issue of buy-in was not necessarily about their knowledge or lack of knowledge (for example, most of us have the knowledge of what a healthy snack is, but we don't always choose a healthy snack). The lack of buy-in was more about the teachers' own beliefs, perceptions, and values (e.g., the belief – "what I am doing is just fine"). This is noted in research which showed one of the major barriers to collaborative work in gifted education was conflicting assumptions between classroom teachers and gifted education teachers. Many classroom teachers had the assumption that gifted students are simply fine on their own and that classroom teachers perceive that they already adequately challenge gifted students (Mofield, 2020a).

You may still be wondering, "Well, what changes their perceptions? What changes their beliefs?" This is the million dollar question! We don't actually have a magic wand to change how people think. However, based on what we know from coaching literature, there are key elements that facilitate buy-in. We have discussed many of these elements throughout this book:

+ Using elements of SCARF in coaching interactions (i.e., status, certainty, autonomy, relatedness, and fairness).
+ Leveraging relationships.
+ Building teacher self-efficacy and collective efficacy (by linking teacher behavior to student outcomes).
+ Understanding models of change (e.g., ADKAR model) and creating contexts where teachers realize an awareness and desire for the change (i.e., Set a Purpose Stage 1 of the Coaching Circuit).
+ Staying curious about their perspectives and beliefs, leveraging a teacher's expertise and values (see Chapter 3).

Three-Pronged Focus (Relationships, Process, Results)

Research from the literature on literacy coaching provides important insight on building buy-in for working with a coach (e.g., Cutrer, 2016). The first approach is to focus on leveraging *relationships* to foster connection. The foundations of mutual trust and respect set the context for effective teacher-coach partnerships. The second approach is to use *"process"* where the coach is intentionally explicit in showing how to use a reading intervention step-by-step so that the teacher is well-prepared to apply the strategy independently. The third approach is to rely on *results*. Through the coaching process, the coach explicitly links the intervention to the student outcomes so the teachers clearly understand how their actions tie directly to student learning.

Cutrer (2016) found that one approach alone is not effective, but when coaches use multiple approaches (relationships, process, and results) teachers were less likely to resist coaching. We find this study highly relevant to GT coaching because the GT Coaching Circuit embodies all three approaches. Positive *relationships* are nurtured through reflective feedback, presuming positive intent, and considering SCARF in all interactions. For *process*, the GT Coaching Circuit provides opportunities to set the teacher up for success in using effective instructional strategies in the Plan and Act stage (see Chapter 5). Further, the *results* approach comes into play when the coach has opportunities to link the teacher's action to student outcomes in the Reflect stage (see Chapter 6).

Recruiting Connectors

In the book *Tipping Point*, Malcolm Gladwell (2002) describes why some ideas spread among large numbers of people and some do not. He explains that it is not simply "word of mouth" of a good idea that causes a number of people to buy-in; rather, it is that the right person (the "connector"), hears about the idea and spreads the word. Connectors are people whose personalities are simply contagious. You can apply this principle to GT coaching by recruiting the most well-respected, influential teachers of the school to work with you for the first year.

Teachers who are parents of gifted students (or any child who needs differentiated instruction) may also be more willing to receive coaching. These teachers already understand the rationale for why differentiation is necessary for special populations; therefore, they may be more willing to be involved in learning more about how to implement these practices in the classroom. When teachers share that their own children are gifted and they understand the need for differentiated instruction in the regular education classroom, this is an excellent opportunity to leverage the relationship to launch into a coaching conversation.

Follow-Up from Professional Learning

One of the most opportune times to follow-up with coaching is after a quality professional learning session. Teachers are often excited to use newly learned strategies in their classroom, especially if the content was presented well and in such a way that teachers feel equipped to immediately use the information. When teachers see themselves as capable and realize, "This is not that hard!" they are eager to put the practices into place. Offering to co-plan with teachers one-on-one or even in teams (see discussion later in this chapter) directly after quality professional learning can be another way to launch GT coaching at your school with buy-in.

Collective Efficacy

One of the most impactful ways to create buy-in is to consider the powerful idea of collective efficacy. Collective efficacy refers to the shared belief that through collective action, teachers can have a direct impact on student outcomes and improve achievement for all students (Donohoo, 2017). Hattie's (2017) visible learning research shows that collective efficacy is the number one factor that affects student achievement. With an effect size of 1.57 (.80+ is considered a large effect), this is more impactful than feedback, student prior knowledge, and student socio-economic status.

We believe this is a critical factor to consider in the context of GT coaching. Through cultivated collective efficacy, teachers perceive how their actions lead to improved outcomes for all students, including gifted and high-potential students. Through establishing collective efficacy, teachers see themselves as key players in all students' success. This means the GT teacher is not seen as solely responsible for teaching gifted students in a pull-out setting, rather, all teachers would perceive a shared responsibility.

Collective efficacy is based on the idea that teachers use evidence to link their actions (i.e., instructional decisions) to student learning. Through measuring student learning, it is an opportunity for teachers to consider, "What does it look like for every student, no matter what their readiness level, to make a year's growth in learning? What does this look like for a student who has already mastered grade-level standards? What does this look like for a twice-exceptional student who needs support in reading but has advanced reasoning skills?" Through collective inquiry, teachers search for high-yield strategies. This, indeed, sets the stage for a GT coach to play a key role in facilitating instructional decision-making as part of a collective effort.

If collective efficacy is so powerful, how do schools create it, and how does this fit with GT coaching? The work of Donohoo (2017) has shown there are 6 enabling conditions for collective efficacy. While these are not "causes" of collective efficacy, they are associated conditions. These are shown in Table 7.1

where we link these conditions to GT coaching. As teachers establish and work towards goals that focus on all students, it is an opportunity to establish the *awareness* and *desire* (from the ADKAR change model) regarding how gifted/ high-potential students fit within the goals.

TABLE 7.1
Six Enabling Conditions of Collective Efficacy Linked to GT Coaching

6 Enabling Conditions of Collective Efficacy	Connection to GT Coaching
1. **Advanced teacher influence**	Teachers have opportunities to contribute to decision making within the school. Related to GT coaching, if the vision is for all students to succeed, then teachers are also a part of making decisions on how this is achieved for gifted and high-potential students. The GT coach can help facilitate decision making for how this is done: "How do you see this working with your students?"
2. **Goal consensus**	Teachers reach a consensus for goals and outcomes. In PLCs or other teams, teachers use data to determine next steps for reaching goals together. Teachers are on the same page about goals to improve outcomes for all students.
3. **Teacher's knowledge about on another's work**	Teachers gain confidence in their own ability to impact student learning as they learn about other teachers' practices. In PLCs, teachers can share how their use of differentiation, use of high-level thinking strategies, depth and complexity, etc. impact student learning.
4. **Cohesive staff**	Teachers are on the same page about important educational aims. There is a shared understanding that teachers are responsible for facilitating learning of all students. GT students are not simply served in a pull-out classroom.
5. **Responsiveness of leadership**	Leaders show respect and concern for staff. The administration provides support to the GT coach articulated on the Connected Gifted Planning Guide.
6. **Effective systems of intervention**	While Donohoo's work uses "intervention" to ensure all students are successful. We propose that this is expanded to advanced academic interventions through differentiation or enrichment so that all students, including gifted/high-potential students, progress in their learning.

Adapted from Donohoo (2017).

Donohoo (2017) refers to effective systems for interventions as the sixth enabling condition. We see this as an opportunity to also consider effective advanced academic interventions (e.g., additional challenge, differentiation, etc.). Response-to-Intervention and Multi-tiered Systems of Supports (MTSS) are models that are often used to align general education curriculum to gifted programming. These models emphasize the need for "intervention" at both ends of the spectrum of student learning (i.e., both remediation and advanced academics) in response to student readiness. Some schools use the term "upper-vention" to describe interventions needed to address any mismatch between the learner's need and instruction (Work, 2014). If students have already demonstrated mastery of grade-level material, they present an academic need that should be eliminated through advanced academic interventions (Peters and Matthews, 2016). A GT coach can help facilitate an application of a model such as this, emphasizing that "beyond regular work" is not just more work, but "different" work. The GT coach might also co-think ideas with teachers for providing extra challenge and intense interventions for students whose needs are not met through Tier I curriculum. Whether your school context uses RTI, MTSS, or a talent development approach to gifted education, we emphasize that GT coaching is applicable to various program models as it supports a teacher in making decisions on facilitating student growth to next levels of learning.

Professional Learning Communities

Collective efficacy can be cultivated through teacher communities such as Professional Learning Communities (PLCs). When implemented in a genuine fashion, they are characterized as "explicitly or implicitly being about shared values and vision, a focus on student learning, taking an inquiry stance, making teaching more public, sharing experiences and expertise, willingness to experiment with alternative strategies, and engaging in reflective dialogue" (Owen, 2014, p. 58).

Though there are a number of PLC models, we discuss Dufour et al.'s (2010) model here to show an entry point for GT coaching. Their framework focuses on helping students achieve at a high level by considering these four questions:

1) What do we want students to learn?
2) How will we know if each student has learned it?
3) How will we respond when some students do not learn it?
4) How can we extend and enrich the learning for students who have demonstrated proficiency (Owen, 2014, p. 99)?

The last question is a prime opportunity to engage as a co-thinking partner with teachers to discuss continuous learning for high-achieving students. The data is used to substantiate a need for a change in instruction. This opens the door to consider flexible grouping, tiered assignments, and other forms of differentiation. As a GT coach, you may have an opportunity to present a strategy during the PLC and then later follow-up about its use in team coaching (see the following section) or individual coaching.

Collective efficacy is not developed from discussing curriculum; rather, it is cultivated when teachers link instructional decisions to student outcomes. This is why GT coaching is so important as a follow-up to what is discussed in PLC meetings. The GT Coaching Circuit allows for reflection on how the strategies did indeed impact how students make continual progress on their learning, even if they had already mastered content. The circuit also allows for an opportunity to discuss how these learning experiences may have allowed the teacher to "spot talent" among high-potential students not formally identified for gifted services.

Unfortunately, PLCs are sometimes regarded by the teacher as being only *contrived* collaboration because teachers are required to participate. If teachers perceive them as "one more thing" they must do, this indeed presents a barrier to a genuine practice of inquiry. The PLC structure may involve teachers "going through the motions" of examining student data without focusing on how to *use* the data to enhance student learning. We bring this up to simply acknowledge that PLCs play out differently across various districts and contexts. Not all PLCs include authentic reflective dialogue as intended by its design. As a GT coach, you can look for entry points to ignite such reflection by asking questions such as, "How can we ensure all students have opportunities to continue to progress in their learning?" You must not underestimate your role as a catalyst for change in questioning the *status quo* to prompt new ideas for student learning, especially for gifted/high-potential students.

Coaching Teams

Beyond co-thinking with teachers in PLCs, there may be other opportunities to collaborate with teachers on grade-level teams or content-based teams. These meetings are also opportunities for GT coaching. The benefit of this is that you can now harness a collective energy where multiple teachers interact and construct knowledge though this may not be as individualized as one-on-one coaching. The GT Coaching Circuit is easily modified to use with a group of teachers.

For example, you may work with a group of teachers to present a mini professional learning session on using pre-assessments. You might work through the steps of "Set a Purpose" to evaluate the need with the group of teachers. You might ask the group, "What do you know about student readiness levels? How do you know what they need to progress in their learning?" Then, facilitate the conversation to articulate a goal established by the group. Members of the team could brainstorm ideas together for reaching the goal. As the group reaches a consensus on a strategy to focus on as a group, you could model the strategy in the group session or guide the teachers through a group co-planning session, where you offer immediate feedback and support. As the teachers are set up for success, they could then implement the strategy in their own classrooms and come back to the group meeting with student work. The team could discuss how the strategy extended student learning, allowed opportunities for problem-solving, or provided opportunities for students to "think like an expert." The coaching sequence remains the same though the circuit revolves around a team goal rather than an individual's.

Coaching a team could be a first step in establishing your role and developing trusting relationships with classroom teachers. After leading a team through a coaching circuit, a teacher may be more willing to engage in one-on-one coaching to focus on a specific skill. Individualized coaching may be a follow-up step from the team coaching.

Before diving into team coaching, it is important to establish norms for the team through a consensus process. These norms will establish certainty (i.e., C in SCARF) and build a foundation of underlying trust. We provide a few suggestions for norms here:

We agree to:

+ Listen respectfully to one another's ideas.
+ Be present in the moment.
+ Presume positive intent.
+ Be aware of own personal impact on others.

These norms can be revisited over time as the teams continue to meet.

A Path Towards Equity

As previously mentioned, GT coaching should align with district initiatives and goals. Many districts prioritize equity initiatives to provide high academic standards to all students. Students from racially, culturally, linguistically, and economically diverse backgrounds are often underrepresented in gifted programs. GT coaching can serve to provide more equitable access to rigorous learning experiences and so lead to more equitable opportunities to be identified as gifted.

For example, a GT coach builds awareness of gifted characteristics and behaviors among students from diverse backgrounds. Further, as a GT coach supports teachers in learning strategies for high-level advanced instruction, this presents more opportunities for all students to engage in robust learning experiences. This leads to contexts where needs of gifted students are not only addressed, but talent is revealed through students engaging with challenging content and showing evidence of insightful connections, creative thinking, and problem-solving abilities.

We have recently worked with a school district who used GT coaching as part of GT programming. The district expanded GT services to identify and serve high-potential students (known as the "Advanced Scholars Cohort") who were not officially identified as "gifted." As part of this program, the GT teachers taught both identified gifted students and "Advanced Scholars Cohort" students in pull-out settings (though in separate groups). Additionally, the GT teachers served as GT coaches by collaborating with and coaching classroom teachers to enhance differentiation and rigorous instruction in the regular education classroom. The goals of this program are shared in Box 7.1.

Though this is only a pilot program for the district, they have found positive outcomes regarding increased identification of gifted students in Title 1 schools, especially in cases when collaboration, coaching, and differentiation were consistently used. For example, in one school, gifted identification increased by 61% (from 13 to 21 students). In this particular circumstance, the administrative support, structure of class schedules, and time to collaborate with teachers were important contributing factors. While this level of increase was not seen across all pilot schools, we are learning more about the contextual supports and structures that are needed to facilitate successful collaborative coaching work.

Box 7.1 Gifted Programming Plan Incorporating GT Coaching with Collaboration

Overview

The Advanced Scholars Cohort initiative is for Advanced Academic learners who show potential to be identified as Gifted and Talented. The program will begin the process of implementing an acceleration of services as an effort to increase rigor and instruction in the General Education classroom through collaboration and differentiation. There will be two types of Advanced Learner Programs. One will be the Gifted and Talented Scholars. The other will be the Advanced Scholars Cohort. The GT Specialist will service both programs. We also want to increase teacher knowledge and proficiency in providing higher level thinking skills and real-world applications to all of our Advanced Learners as applied to the Texas TEKS.

Goals and Benefits

1. Identifying and challenging advanced learners who are not receiving services for the Gifted Program. These may be students who meet or master their grade level academically or advanced learners in each grade level.
2. Increased academic outcomes for student learners.
3. Increased differentiation in the general education classroom setting that is more student lead than teacher lead and provides rigor.
4. Enhances students' reasoning, critical thinking, and real world connection skills.
5. Allow Gifted Teachers an opportunity to learn more about curriculum content and connect it more to gifted programming.
6. Teacher and student accountability as well as shared responsibility.
7. Participate in the pull-out/push in model for Advanced Academic Support.
8. Students in the Advanced Scholars Cohort will not be pulled at the same time as the Gifted Learners.

Preparing a Path for Successful Collaboration

+ Learning how to communicate using collaboration
+ Using professional learning in collaboration, co-planning, and co-teaching
+ Volunteer participation and incentives for students
+ If possible, we would like to utilize the cluster grouping concept (GT/Cohort students with one general education teacher) This would prevent having to utilize too many teachers and resources.
+ Initial identification methods are campus-based assessments, Star 360, Schoolzilla, and teacher recommendation or referral into the Scholars Program.
+ Clear expectations on using the differentiation framework.

Launching Program Essentials

1. Implement Co-Planning and Collaboration for the first nine weeks

2. Clustering students
   a. Choose a teacher to cluster the Cohort/GT students with. Ensure they have training in gifted and talented (i.e., initial 30 hours or update courses)
   b. At least 6 students in a class with a maximum of 9 Scholars/GT students (with collaboration from the GT Specialist and chosen classroom teacher.
3. Schedule planning time for General Education teacher and GT Specialist to collaborate (at least 30 minutes weekly).
   a. Scheduling can include time in the PLC for Planning, or the teacher/GT specialist can meet during planning periods (Zoom meetings are an option if needed). Self-paced professional development opportunities will be available.
   b. Reviewing schedules for push-in or pull out for our Twice Exceptional students who may be in the Dyslexia Program, Bilingual Program, or Special Education.
   c. A Collaborative Process Model will be given to the teachers as a resource for how they should collaborate during planning.
   d. Open a shared drive for lesson plans so teachers can view the lesson plans and determine the pacing and TEKS. Teachers can also share ideas and resources for differentiation. Identify clear roles and expectations.

Supports Provided

+ Professional development opportunities.
+ Sending out communication to parents (i.e., newsletters, parent nights, and parent conferences, parent permission request, and any GT/Scholar assessment tools).
+ Coaching sessions provided by experts in the field with the GT specialist.
+ Reflection and feedback opportunities using google forms, surveys, GT specialist PLCs, and visits from the GT facilitator.
+ Learning how to collaborate effectively/help enhance leadership/ and set goals around effective differentiation using the TTESS framework.

Developed by Tina Moore and Zenobia Denny (from Moore & Denny, 2022).

Cultivating Resilience

Sometimes working in gifted education can feel like an uphill battle. Undoubtedly, there will be times that you have to step out of your comfort zone into vulnerability. You may also feel like you are alone on an island because other teachers simply do not hold the same beliefs about teaching gifted/high-potential students as you. Further, teaching is a difficult profession, especially within recent years; teachers' plates are simply full to the brim. It is difficult for anyone to have the desire to grow professionally when in survival mode. The reality is that not all teachers will want to engage with you in coaching, and this can feel like personal rejection. In these cases, it is important to realize what is within your control and what is outside of your control. You cannot control another teacher's attitude or behavior, but you can come to work with passion and enthusiasm for advocating that all students progress in their learning, including gifted and high-potential students. Every time you reach out to work with another teacher is a moment of vulnerability, but through this vulnerability you have an opportunity to develop courage and strength.

As a GT coach that serves as a catalyst for change, you will likely be challenging the *status quo* at many levels. Not everyone will embrace these changes to day-to-day practices. How will you feel when other teachers do not get on board with you? Do you interpret this as failure, or can you move forward with what you can control? Seligman's (2006) work explains that people perceive failure through two different lenses. The pessimistic view is that failure is *permanent* (i.e., it's like this forever), *pervasive* (i.e., it seeps into other areas), and *personal* (i.e., it's all my fault). The learned optimism view, by contrast, is that the situation can change, this is just one instance of failure, and the failure is not entirely personal (other elements are at play beyond one's control). Those who adopt learned optimism are more likely to persist through difficulty with resilience. The next time you experience a setback within your coaching experiences, you might reframe your thoughts with a dose of learned optimism. Here, we share a mantra:

> It's this situation, this time.
> Things can change, I will rise.
> Is this something I can control?
> What I cannot, I will let go.
> Mofield (2020b).

Collaborate to Advocate

As you step into the deep waters of collaboration and coaching, remember that every interaction and conversation is an opportunity to advocate for gifted and high-potential students. These students are one of the most underserved and misunderstood populations in schools. As a GT coach you are opening doors for gifted/high-potential students with every question you ask and every strategy you share. So, consider, what questions do these students need you to ask? What actions do they need you to take? As you reflect on your sphere of influence, remember you advocate when you collaborate! We are excited for you as you catalyze change in your role as a GT coach. For gifted and high-potential students, you are a key catalyst in transforming potential into realized talent!

Reflection Questions

1) From your administrator's point of view, what goals are prioritized at your school? How does GT coaching fit with these goals? What are your next steps in communicating your role and vision for GT coaching at your school?
2) Consider the contexts of collaborative teams at your school. To what extent does genuine collaboration occur vs. contrived collaboration? How can you tell the difference?
3) Among the 6 enabling conditions of collective efficacy, to what extent are they present at your school?
4) What are the greatest challenges you have experienced with "buy-in"? What successes have you had in building buy-in with those you work with?
5) In what ways do you see your role as a catalyst for change in your context?

References

Cutrer, E. (2016). *The benefit of literacy coaching for initial resistance to implementation of a literacy program for struggling readers* (Doctoral dissertation). *https://doi.org/10.17615/smjb-gq92.*

Donohoo, J. (2017). *Collective efficacy: How educators' beliefs impact student learning.* Corwin.

DuFour, R., DuFour, R., Eaker, R., & Many, T. (2010*). Learning by doing: A handbook for professional learning communities at work* (2nd ed.). Solution Tree Press.

Gladwell, M. (2002). *The tipping point: How little things can make a big difference.* Back Bay Books.

Hattie, J. (2017). Visible learning MetaX. https://www.visiblelearningmetax.com/Influences.

Mofield, E. L. (2020a). Benefits and barriers to collaboration and co-teaching: Examining perspectives of gifted education teachers and general education teachers. *Gifted Child Today, 43*(1), 20–33. https://doi.org/10.1177/1076217519880588.

Mofield, E. (2020b). Teaching psychosocial skills and habits of achievement. In P. Olszewski-Kubilius, P., & T. Stambaugh, T. *Supporting students from low-income families.* Prufrock Press.

Mofield, E. (2023). *Vertical differentiation for gifted, advanced, and high-potential students: 25 strategies to stretch student thinking.* Routledge Press.

Moore, T., & Denny, Z. (2022*). Advanced scholars cohort (ASC) program* [Unpublished manuscript]. Department of GT/Advanced Academics, Grand Prairie Independent School District.

Owen, S. (2014). Teacher professional learning communities: going beyond contrived collegiality toward challenging debate and collegial learning and professional growth. *Australian Journal of Adult Learning, 54*(2), 54+. https://link.gale.com/apps/doc/A379090591/AONE?u=tel_oweb&sid=googleScholar&xid=ba9d95f8.

Peters, S. J., & Matthews, M.S. (2016). An advanced academics approach to curriculum building. In Kettler, T. (Ed.) *Modern curriculum for gifted and advanced students* (p. 55–67). Prufrock Press.

Seligman, M. (2006*). Learned optimism: How to change your mind and your life.* Vintage Books.

Work, J. (2014, May 20). Uppervention: Meeting the needs of gifted and talented students. Edutopia. https://www.edutopia.org/blog/uppervention-for-gifted-talented-students-josh-work.

Appendix A

GT Coaching Circuit and Coaching Notes

Set a Purpose	Plan and Act	Reflect
Establish a student-focused goal	Select and learn a strategy	Reflect on student learning and next steps

Set a Purpose — Establish a student-focused goal

Evaluate Need
Determine Need: As you think about the gifted/high-potential students in your classroom
+ What do you know about their readiness levels? Strengths?
+ What do they need to progress in their learning? How do you know?
+ What are their next steps in learning?
+ On a scale from 1–10, how well do you think___? Why did you not say 1? What would it take for you to feel more confident?
+ When you think about challenging every student in the classroom, what gets in the way?

Establish Goal
+ Goal- What are you wanting students to do and understand?
+ Criteria- What might this look like?
+ Baseline- Where are students already in relation to this goal?

Explore Ideas
Create a Focus Question
+ In what ways might___? How might students___?
Brainstorm
+ What ideas do you have already?
+ Would you like to brainstorm ideas together?

Plan and Act — Select and learn a strategy

Select a Strategy
Choose a strategy to implement, considering its purpose and impact on student outcomes.
+ How does the desired student outcome align with the purpose of the strategy?
+ How does the strategy engage gifted and high-potential students as a means to increase academic achievement and student growth?
+ How does the strategy provide opportunities for students to make connections, problem-solve, or accelerate their learning?

Use the Tool Template: *What, Why, How*
Elicit teacher input with GT Instructional Blueprint:
+ How do you think you might modify this with your students?

Support the Teacher in Learning the Strategy
Discuss options for co-action:
+ Model the strategy (bite-sized modeling).
+ Co-teach the strategy through a shared vision.
+ Co-plan a lesson with the teacher.

Set up for Success
When the teacher is ready, the teacher uses the strategy in own planning and instruction. Provide reflective feedback on use of strategy (if requested).

Reflect — Reflect on student learning and next steps

Reflect on Goal Attainment
Revisit the Goal
+ What was the goal? To what extent did students achieve it?
Reflect on Evidence
+ How did the selected strategy impact gifted and high-potential students? Other students? Reveal talent and recognize student strengths?
+ In what ways did you observe students showing creative thinking? Critical thinking? Making connections?, etc.

Reflect on Building Capacity
Make connections between student outcomes and teacher decisions
+ When you did___, what did you notice from students?

Reflect Forward
Celebrate
Transfer to new contexts
+ How might this strategy be used in other content areas? with a different group of students? in an upcoming unit?
Revise Goal/Plan Next Steps
+ What are your next steps?
+ Do you want to revise the goal?
+ When can we meet again?

Set a Purpose	Coaching Notes	Coaching Prompts
Establish a Student-Focused Goal **Evaluate Need** Determine Need: As you think about the gifted/high-potential students in your classroom + What do you know about their readiness levels? strengths? + What do they need to progress in their learning? How do you know? + What are their next steps in learning? + On a scale from 1–10, how well do you think ___? Why did you not say 1? What would it take for you to feel more confident? + When you think about challenging every student in the classroom, what gets in the way? **Establish Goal** + Goal- What are you wanting students to do and understand? + Criteria- What might this look like? + Baseline- Where are students already in relation to this goal? **Explore Ideas** Create a Focus Question + In what ways might ___? How might students ___? Brainstorm + What ideas do you have already? + Would you like to brainstorm ideas together?	Goal:	+ What do you want to focus on? + You value ___. It's exciting to see ___. + What would happen if ___? + I'm curious about that . . . + Tell me more . . . + So, in other words ___? Is that right? + So, you are saying ___. + You are wanting students to . . .

Plan and Act	Coaching Notes	Coaching Prompts
Select and Learn a Strategy		+ *What do you want to focus on?*
		+ *You value____. It's exciting to see____.*
Select a Strategy		+ *What would happen if____?*
Choose a strategy to implement, considering its purpose and impact on student outcomes.		+ *I'm curious about that . . .*
+ *How does the desired student outcome align with the purpose of the strategy?*		+ *Tell me more . . .*
+ *How does the strategy engage gifted and high-potential students as a means to increase academic achievement and student growth?*		+ *So, in other words____? Is that right?*
+ *How does the strategy provide opportunities for students to make connections, problem-solve, or accelerate their learning?*		+ *So, you are saying____.*
Use the Tool Template: *What, Why, How*		
Elicit teacher input with GT Instructional Blueprint:		
+ *How do you think you might modify this with your students?*		
Support the Teacher in Learning the Strategy		
Discuss options for co-action:		
+ Model the strategy (bite-sized modeling).		
+ Co-teach the strategy through a shared vision.		
+ Co-plan a lesson with the teacher.		
Set up for Success		
When the teacher is ready, the teacher uses the strategy in own planning and instruction.		
Provide reflective feedback on use of strategy (if requested).		

Reflect	Coaching Notes	Coaching Prompts
Reflect on student learning and next steps **Reflect on Goal Attainment** Revisit the Goal + *What was the goal? To what extent did students achieve it?* Reflect on Evidence + *How did the selected strategy impact gifted and high-potential students? Other students? Reveal talent and recognize student strengths?* + *In what ways did you observe students showing creative thinking? Critical thinking? Making connections?, etc.* **Reflect on Building Capacity** Make connections between student outcomes and teacher decisions + *When you did this____, what did you notice from students?* **Reflect Forward** Celebrate Transfer to new contexts + *How might this strategy be used in other content areas? with a different group of students? in an upcoming unit?* Revise Goal/Plan Next Steps + *What are your next steps?* + *Do you want to revise the goal?* + *When can we meet again?*		+ *What do you want to focus on?* + *You value____. It's exciting to see____.* + *Would happen if___?* + *I'm curious about that . . .* + *Tell me more . . .* + *So, in other words____? Is that right?* + *So, you are saying___.*

Appendix B

Coaching Scenario

Context for Coaching Session

The following scenario portrays a coaching session that takes place following a school professional learning session. The GT coach is working with a 4th grade classroom teacher. The GT coach and teacher have previously had small discussions about several students in the class, so the coach has a general understanding of the classroom context. Throughout this coaching scenario, the GT coach uses the coaching notes to record the teacher-selected goal and any additional co-thinking or insights that stem from the coaching conversation. The flexibility of the coaching circuit allows the GT coach to adapt to the needs of the teacher to ensure purposeful and reflective dialogue. Within this session, the coaching circuit provides an opportunity to address several areas concurrently as they organically evolve through reflective dialogue.

SET A PURPOSE STAGE

GT Coach: I'm so glad that we were able to find a time to talk a little bit more about our recent professional learning session on differentiation. In talking with you briefly after the session, you had mentioned that you are wanting to differentiate more for your gifted and high-potential students in your class. I remember you telling me how you might want to possibly even try a few of the shared strategies in your class. Is that right?

Teacher: Yes, I'm realizing that I have some really advanced learners, and I feel like I need to do more. I thought that session was really good, but there was just *so much* information that it feels a little overwhelming to me. I really don't know where to start.

GT Coach: Well, let me start by asking, based on what we learned in that session, if you had to rate your current use of differentiation for gifted learners on a scale from 1–10 (10 being the highest and 1 being lowest), what number would you give?

Teacher: Hmmm . . . . well, I know that I want all of my students to learn, and I make sure to provide a lot of choice in their learning, but after today, I learned that differentiation goes way beyond providing choice. I think I now realize I have to think about how I can integrate deeper levels of thinking into choice. I guess I would just give myself a "3."

GT Coach: Thank you for being so reflective in your rating. With this "3" you recognize the opportunity to grow and learn through this process. Let's reflect a little bit more. What aspects of your teaching set you apart from a "1"?

Teacher: I think I see that students have different learning needs, and meeting those needs are a key part of my teaching philosophy, but I heard that lady talking today, and I just started feeling so overwhelmed, and quite honestly, I don't even know where to start.

GT Coach: It is clear how much you value meeting the needs of your students. As we continue to narrow down a focus on how to support you in this task, let's think back to your rating. What do you think it would take for you to grow from a 3?

Teacher: I just don't know how to start! That's why I'm here! [nervous giggle]

GT Coach: Well, let me ask you . . . which part of the professional learning session stands out in your memory the most? What really resonated with you?

Teacher: Hmmm . . . there was so much information, but what I felt most connected to was tiered instruction . . . and those icons. What were they called?

GT Coach: Oh, yes! Those are Kaplan's depth and complexity icons. Sometimes we like to refer to the icons as thinking tools because they give students the needed tools to process information. When you think about the two differentiation strategies you mentioned, tiering and the depth and complexity thinking tools, what are your initial thoughts about incorporating these in instruction?

Teacher: Well, [The teacher pauses, and the coach gives time for the teacher to process without interjecting any new questions. After an appropriate amount of time, the teacher begins to share.] I think I could probably work that into what I already do with my students, like in centers. I think there's probably a way for the centers to be bumped up, so they aren't just doing something different, but that they are also truly going to grow in their learning.

GT Coach: So, it sounds like you are wanting students to have differentiated center assignments that stretch them in their thinking. Does that sound about right?

Teacher: Yes, for sure!

GT Coach: You mentioned that you would like to see students grow in their thinking. What would that look like?

Teacher: When I think about academic growth, I would want to see my students' responses have more depth and be better supported with evidence. I do not want my students to just give basic knowledge responses. I really want them to stretch their thinking through appropriately challenging assignments.

GT Coach: Great! I think you've just identified your goal. *Students will stretch their thinking through appropriately challenging assignments.* You also said you want them to show more depth with evidence. So, let's write down your goal: ***Students will stretch their thinking through appropriately challenging assignments.*** We will be able to see this when students produce evidence to support their thinking [criteria]. You mentioned earlier that your students are currently given choice in their center activities, but you would like to add deeper levels of thinking to those center activities. What ideas do you have to achieve this goal or would you like suggestions?

Teacher: Hmmm . . . like I said earlier . . . I would really like to use what we learned at that professional learning session. I would like to do something with tiering and the thinking tools, but I don't know how. I would appreciate any suggestions!

PLAN AND ACT STAGE

[Because this coaching session is stemming from strategies learned from a professional learning session, the teacher has already clearly indicated a desire to implement tiering and the depth and complexity thinking tools as selected strategies. With the flexibility of the coaching circuit, the GT coach is able to proceed with the other aspects of the Plan and Act stage as follows.]

GT Coach: Before we think about different options of using tiering and the thinking tools together, let me first ask you how you might know which students would need which tiered level of instruction?

Teacher: Well, I do use the quarterly benchmark scores to know how to group my students. We talk about where students are in their readiness levels in our PLCs. So, I am already using that to create the groups. But I don't always do different things with my groups, even though my advanced learners sometimes have different texts. Anyways, I do use benchmarks! [smiles]

GT Coach: It's nice to see how you already place an emphasis on understanding the different learning needs of your students. As we work towards meeting your goal, it is important that we recognize the purpose behind the tiering and the thinking tools as instructional strategies to make sure that they align with your goal. In thinking back to what we learned at our session, what aspects of tiering and the thinking tools do you see supporting your goal?

Teacher: Well, because tiering focuses on students' readiness levels, I think that really fits with my goal, and I really like the thinking tools because they seem to open up so many possibilities for differentiation. I know they could be used to challenge my gifted students, but I definitely need help with understanding exactly how.

GT Coach: Yes, understanding "why" a strategy is used and "how" a strategy is used are integral in our instructional decision-making. When we think about the "why", or purpose, for using depth and complexity thinking tools, we know that the thinking tools provide opportunities for students to examine data and make connections within and across disciplines. In what ways do you see this supporting your goal? [Coach references the written goal on the coaching notes for the teacher to reference if needed.]

Teacher: That totally supports how students can be stretched in their thinking. I could really think through how my center activities could provide opportunities for students to make connections through advanced content.

GT Coach: Yes, you are applying the purpose of the strategy to the desired student outcomes! I think you have just refined your goal even more by including that students will be making connections through appropriately challenging assignments. Let's write down that refined goal: **Students will stretch their thinking by making connections through appropriately challenging assignments.**

This helps us know specifically what we are looking for in our student outcomes. We also know that you want them to use evidence to support their thinking. Now we need to explore "how" the strategy works. In a nutshell, the thinking tools can be used to guide students to examine content through the lens of a disciplinarian. Because you know that you would like to use this strategy to achieve your goal, let's go ahead and take a closer look at "how" the strategy is used within the classroom. [The coach pulls out the Tool Template: Resource 5.3; Chapter 5.] This Tool Template will help us talk through the different steps in using the depth and complexity thinking tools, and this understanding will help us once we start co-thinking options for how they can be used in your centers. [The GT coach now completes the Tool Template alongside the teacher, filling in the *what*, *why*, and *how* sections of the resource. While working through the key steps, the GT coach and teacher reference the ABC's of Differentiation as appropriate for the given context.]

Teacher: This totally makes sense. It's nice to see it broken down like this. I feel like the thinking tools are exactly what I want to use in working towards my goal. [Teacher looks at clock.] Oh, it's almost time for me to go pick up my class from related arts.

GT Coach: OK, let's go ahead and set a time that we can meet again. [The GT coach and teacher schedule their next meeting.]
[The GT coach and teacher resume their coaching conversation from the previous meeting.]

GT Coach: [The GT coach and teacher exchange pleasantries, and the GT coach places the coaching notes and the Tool Template on the table to reference as needed alongside the teacher.] I've been looking forward to continuing our conversation! As we co-think how this strategy will support you in meeting your goal, let's take a closer look at how this strategy can be used within your classroom. [The GT coach shows the teacher the GT Instructional Blueprint.] This GT Instructional Blueprint will guide us through some additional considerations of how students can be "stretched" in their thinking through this strategy. This Blueprint gives us the space to co-construct how high leverage practices, student agency, and access points for learning can be leveraged within your lesson.

Teacher: Ok, that sounds great, but I have to tell you that I have no idea what high leverage practices are [nervous giggle].

GT Coach: While you may not be familiar with this official name, I have heard you mention several of them in our PLC meetings. High leverage practices are simply instructional practices that enhance or make adjustments to evidence-based instruction. They are considerations like flexible grouping, engaging in metacognition, and providing scaffolds.

Teacher: [relieved] Oh! I do all those things! I just didn't know what they were called! So, this Blueprint is just going to have us talk through how I can use those things with this strategy?

GT Coach: That's absolutely right. There are so many things to think through when we are learning new strategies, so the Blueprint gives us a space to co-construct how this strategy can be used specifically with your classroom context in mind. In addition to high leverage practices, it also has us think through the considerations of student agency and access points, as well.

Teacher: Great! How do we start?

GT Coach: Let's start by me asking you, "In knowing your students, what are your initial ideas of how you would use the depth and complexity thinking tools and tiering in your class?"

Teacher: Well, you know that I am going to be using them in centers, and I think the tiering is going to be the easy part because we can kind of think of creating "levels" for the learning tasks. Because you just told me what high leverage practices are, I'm already thinking about using flexible grouping based on my students' benchmark scores to decide the center rotations. From there, I'm thinking that once I know which thinking tools I am going to use, I can give sentence stems or use visuals to help my students if they need extra support, and maybe at the end, I can have the students do a reflection of "thinking about their thinking" which would engage them in metacognition. Does that work?

GT Coach: Wow! You thought of some nice considerations that will help us in co-planning later! I made sure to write down the ideas that you just shared in the high leverage practice section of the blueprint. You mentioned providing scaffolds for your students. Are there any particular students that you have in mind that might need scaffolds?

Teacher: For sure! I have some students who really struggle, and I have some multilingual learners, too!

GT Coach: What about your gifted students? How might you provide scaffolds for them?

Teacher: Well, I do have two gifted multilingual learners, but my other gifted students always seem to do fine without any extra supports.

GT Coach: Let's double check your goal: **Students will stretch their thinking by making connections through appropriately challenging assignments.** When we think about using advanced content

	to stretch your gifted learners, what areas might they feel challenged enough to need a scaffold as part of differentiating "up"?
Teacher:	Oh, wow! I'm so used to thinking about meeting grade level standards, that I forget that even my gifted learners might need support when working on advanced grade level standards. This really gets me thinking. [Teacher pauses to think.] I think I might need to go over some key vocabulary with them first from any reading material that I might choose . . . maybe I could have some visuals with that, too.
GT Coach:	Great idea. Once we focus more on content, we will have some other ideas, too! What are your thoughts in terms of student agency and access points?
Teacher:	It's funny, when I see the high leverage practices that I mentioned, it makes me think of how scaffolds also provide access points for my multilingual learners, and then I think about how scaffolds give them greater independence in their learning, and that makes me think about agency. As I'm talking this through with you, I'm also thinking about our unit on biographies and how I can incorporate biographies of people that share common backgrounds with my students . . . . like, I need to make sure that I have culturally responsive materials for my students to connect to. I really hadn't thought about that until just now. Wow! This Blueprint really gets me thinking!
GT Coach:	That's great! It's wonderful to hear your ideas and how you are so student-centered in your thinking. [The GT coach and teacher continue in their coaching conversation specific to the learning needs of the teacher's classroom. The GT coach might also ask, "When considering the ABC's of Differentiation, how will high leverage practices, access points, and agency further support/extend student learning?" [As part of this conversation, the GT coach could refer back to the teacher's *aha* moment of recognizing the need for additional scaffolds to differentiate "up" (as part of the ABCs) for some students. This reference could open further dialogue for other connections focused on HLPs, student agency, and access points.] The coach might also use questions as outlined in Chapter 5 to guide the coaching conversation. The GT coach and teacher make their co-thinking explicit by recording their shared understandings on the Blueprint for future reference as needed.]
GT Coach:	Now that we have a greater understanding of how this strategy can best be implemented with *your* students and *your* goal, let's begin exploring what specific learning tasks and/or depth and complexity

thinking tools might **stretch student's thinking by making connections through appropriately challenging assignments.** When we met last time, you said you would appreciate suggestions, would you still like some, or do you have some ideas that we can talk through?

Teacher: [smiles] I would still like suggestions, please.

GT Coach: Well, there are a couple of options we could explore. Since we know that we are going to be using the thinking tools in center rotations:

+ We could look at how the thinking tools could be added to the centers you have created to tier those centers.

+ We could look at how you could add the thinking tools to other choice activities through choice boards/menus as an alternative to center rotations.

+ Or we could look at how you could intentionally incorporate the thinking tools with high level thinking questions as students work with you at one of the center rotations.

Teacher: My students are really comfortable with center rotations, so I like the idea of using the thinking tools to make some of the centers more challenging. I think I would really like to focus next steps on which thinking tools to use and how to incorporate them to stretch my students into appropriately challenging activities in their centers.

GT Coach: Alright! You are really focused on your goal here. We can move towards this goal by incorporating depth and complexity thinking tools into tiered station activities. We might want to focus on introducing a few of these for students to master before we add more thinking tools into the mix.

Teacher: Sounds good. I don't want them feeling as overwhelmed as I did when I saw them for the first time.

GT Coach: As we heard at our professional learning session, the thinking tools add greater depth and complexity to learning. Why don't we pick 1 or 2 of the thinking tools from each of these areas? As students are new to this, when we think about adding depth into student learning, I would suggest choosing from: details, language of the discipline, unanswered questions, and ethics. In knowing your students and what content you are currently working on, which *two* of these would you like to focus on?

Teacher: I like the *unanswered questions* because it seems to tap into their curiosities and open doors for new research. I also think *ethics* would be great, especially for my gifted kids, because they love to debate! So, maybe we can go with both of those. [The GT coach writes these down.]

GT Coach: Great! Let's also think about how we can integrate one icon focused on adding complexity. Which of these do you think you would like to focus on: multiple points of view, change over time, or across the disciplines?

Teacher: I think the *change over time* might be good to start with. This might really relate well to their current ELA centers since our unit is on biographies. [The GT coach writes this down.]

GT Coach: Most definitely! You have just made a great connection from the strategy to your content area! From building off of what we learned at our session, these thinking tools also lend themselves to tiering lessons to further meet the needs of gifted learners and add challenge to those in the high-achieving group. For instance, for most of your students, you might just be asking them to find the details in a text, explore the ethical implications of a particular text, or analyze a text through multiple points of view. When we are working to differentiate to challenge gifted learners, or anyone else who needs it, we want to combine and integrate the thinking tools into one guiding task and also make sure they are engaged in high-level thinking. This is an example of how we are addressing the "Create the Challenge" as part of the ABC's of Differentiation. For instance, using the three that I just mentioned, we might ask students to integrate all three of these together by asking a question like, "How might multiple points of view use different details within this text to express their ethical concerns?" [The GT coach writes this down on the coaching notes for the teacher to see and process.] How might you be able to combine the thinking tools that you would like to focus on within your classroom?

Teacher: Got it, so maybe with the short biographies they are reading in the centers, they could do more than just answer the set of questions I have about the person's life. Maybe, "How did the controversies of the time period change over time?" And then, "How did these controversies affect the person?" Oh, wait! This makes me think about what we talked about a minute ago with student agency. If I have students reading biography selections that they can personally relate to, then they will be able to answer these questions better!

GT Coach: Totally! Great connection. The Blueprint is helping you "design" your instructional decision-making! What you just shared would definitely lead your students to your goal of making connections and stretching their thinking through appropriately challenging activities. Before we jump in with developing differentiated center activities for your students, however, it is important for your students to learn what these thinking tools are and how they can be used as thinking tools. Would you like co-teach with me as we introduce them to your students or would you prefer that I come in and model for you how to use these selected thinking tools with your students?

Teacher: I don't think I am ready to dive-in to co-teaching them just yet, but I think I could really benefit from seeing you model them.

GT Coach: Fantastic! Why don't we go ahead and schedule a time for me to model? Maybe over lunch tomorrow, I can talk you through my planning and instructional considerations for the modeled lesson, and you can tell me a little bit more about your students and classroom culture. You can also provide insight to help me connect the lesson to a current unit of study. Then we can schedule a time to come back together to reflect upon what we learned from that modeling session. From there, you could introduce the other thinking tools and have more and more options for tiering some of the center work.

Teacher: That sounds great! Thanks!

[The GT Coach models the lesson and has the teacher complete Resource 5.5: Observing Instructional Strategies for Gifted Learners; Chapter 5. The two reflect after the modeling session about key take-aways as related to the goal and insights gained, and the teacher begins to use the strategy independently in planning and instruction. It is possible during this time that the teacher might request that the GT coach collect additional data during the teacher's implementation of the strategy within the classroom. In these cases, the GT Coach would use Resource 5.6: Data Collection Form: Student Learning and Teacher Actions; Chapter 5. Once the teacher has had the opportunity to independently use the strategy and collect data in regard to student outcomes, the GT Coach and teacher schedule a time to reflect.]

REFLECT STAGE

[The GT coach and teacher exchange pleasantries, and the GT coach pulls out the coaching notes and any other data collection resources that would aid in the reflection process to reference as needed alongside the teacher.]

GT Coach: I've been looking forward to meeting with you today! So, before we dive-in, let's revisit your goal: **Students will stretch their thinking by making connections through appropriately challenging assignments.** As we reflect on your goal and how you implemented it into your instruction, to what extent were students able to achieve the desired student outcomes?

Teacher: I was actually really surprised. I brought some of their work samples to share with you. By looking at these, you can see that most of the students demonstrated some real growth.

[The GT coach and teacher look at the student work samples, and the GT coach is able to ask questions to guide the teacher in reflecting on evidence of student outcomes. The GT coach might ask:

+ In what ways are you able to see students are making connections through these learning tasks?

+ In what ways do these learning tasks represent how students were able to use their strengths?

Additional suggestions are provided in Chapter 6.]

GT Coach: Thank you so much for sharing these work samples and reflecting with me through what you saw in the classroom and what we see as collected evidence. While we both can see that overall, your goal was achieved, I do want to ask a follow-up question. As we were reflecting on the student work samples, you stated that you were a little disappointed that your two gifted multilingual learners did not perform as well as you had hoped. As we reflect on this, what do you think could have been contributing factors for this?

Teacher: I'm not entirely sure. I mean, they heard the same explanations as everyone, and the thinking tools, themselves, have picture clues, and I had sentence stems for how to respond through the thinking tools. In talking with them prior to this learning task, my formative assessments also indicated that they understood the thinking tools and how to use them. If they understood how to use them, I am not sure why they did not have the outcomes I was hoping for. I'm really not sure.

GT Teacher: You share that your formative assessments indicated that they understood the thinking tools. This is important information to have in guiding us in reflecting more on this. How did you assess their background knowledge/funds of knowledge in regard to the content they were going to engage with?

Teacher:	Hmmm . . . I think I was so focused on the thinking tools that I forgot about the content they were connecting to, oh-my! I remember talking about this with you earlier when we talked about scaffolds for differentiating "up." These two students are identified gifted students, so I made sure that they had the advanced reading material, but now I am realizing that I forgot to add in the scaffolds for the above grade level reading they were working from. That would have made a big difference for them.
GT Coach:	That is a powerful insight! Stay with that line of thinking . . . What would you do differently next time?
Teacher:	That's a good question that is really making me think. In my future lessons, I am going to make sure that I have visuals for the advanced vocabulary and that I will go over those words with them prior to giving them the reading. I think I could also give them the option to work in pairs. Actually, the more I think about it, I think I will also use more of a gradual release model in building background content knowledge prior to giving them this above grade-level text. That question really made me think! I usually just think about everything I did wrong instead of what I can do right next time.
GT Coach:	You showed some strong forward reflection there, and now you have some additional ideas for how to support your multilingual gifted students in meeting your goal. It is clear how much you value student learning. You also made a great connection between the student outcomes and instructional decisions. Let's take this a little bit deeper and see if we can make some other connections between the student outcomes and instructional decisions. [The GT coach leads the teacher through the RISE model (see Chapter 6) by asking questions such as:

+ When you asked your students what personally inspired them when reading their biographies, what did you notice from your students?
+ What action(s) from you elicited greater student engagement from gifted and high-potential learners?

From these reflective discussions the GT coach can then bridge the teacher into deeper levels of metacognition by asking questions such as:

+ How have you grown in your own awareness of gifted and high-potential learners?]

GT Coach: Thank you for sharing your reflective insights and personal connections to your instructional practice.

Teacher: This really made me think through my instructional decision-making in a good way. I can see my areas of strength, and I actually feel confident in knowing some small steps I can take to strengthen my areas for growth. I am actually excited to apply some of these take-aways in the unit I am planning right now. It has really opened my eyes to when I am planning to challenge my gifted and high-potential learners that I need to not only provide the scaffolds to the strategies as a means to differentiate "up," I also need to remain mindful of the high leverage practices and access points that we had talked about on the Blueprint. There is a lot to think about, but I feel really empowered to make these changes!

GT Coach: Well, *that* is a celebration! Thank you for sharing your thinking with me. I am excited to hear how your next unit evolves. Would you like to apply your take-aways from this session and create a new goal for your upcoming unit?

Teacher: That would be great! I feel like my last goal was pretty successful with the exception of those two students, and I am wondering if my new goal could focus on creating scaffolds for a new strategy *and* advanced content.

GT Coach: You are already applying your learning to new contexts! This is exciting! I'm glad to be learning beside you on this journey. Let's check our calendars to see when we might be able to meet. Also, if you have any information on your upcoming unit, maybe you could email it to me, so I could be really prepared the next time we meet.

Teacher: That sounds great!

Appendix C

GT Toolkit of Strategies and Thinking Models

The GT Toolkit of Strategies and Thinking Models shows several popular instructional strategies, models, and questioning structures for gifted and high-potential students. This is not an exhaustive list, and we encourage you to create your own toolbox of strategies to share. A strategy is simply the method for how students interact with and learn content. Strategies for gifted students should allow students to generate ideas and promote inquiry by expanding thinking beyond what is known by the learner already (VanTassel-Baska & Baska, 2019).

These tools can be used for differentiating instruction, tiering assignments, developing inquiry-based experiences, and "bumping up" the rigor of questions and other tasks. Here, we provide an outline of these strategies for easy reference, including its purpose and a brief overview of how it is used. This can be a go-to source for a GT coach when:

+ Discussing ideas for extending student learning in PLCs.
+ Providing short professional learning sessions.
+ Planning differentiated assessments and creating differentiated rubrics.
+ Providing options for teachers to use, tailored to the standards and lesson objectives.
+ Modeling/demonstrating strategies for a classroom teacher.
+ Co-planning lesson activities.
+ Creating individual learning experiences for students who "compact out" of regular work.

+ Coaching teachers to select a strategy to use, aligned with their own student-focused goal.
+ Serving as a focus for operationalizing "critical thinking" or "creative thinking."

We share a full list of many recommended resources and evidence-based curriculum materials here:

High-Quality/Evidence-Supported Gifted Curriculum Units
+ University of Connecticut (M^3) Math Curriculum (Kendall Hunt)
+ William and Mary Gifted Curriculum Units (Kendall Hunt and Routledge Press)
+ Vanderbilt Programs for Talented Youth Units (Routledge Press)
+ Gallagher et al. PBL units (from Royal Fireworks Press)
+ University of Virginia CLEAR curriculum units (Routledge Press)
+ Jacob's Ladder Reading Comprehension Series (Routledge Press)

Recommended Resources for Instructional Strategies in Gifted Education
+ Byrd, I., & VanGemert, L. (2019). *Gifted guild's guide to depth and complexity: Finding your way through the framework.* Gifted Guild.
+ Cash, R. (2017). *Advancing differentiation: Thinking and learning for the 21st century.* Free Spirit Press.
+ Center for Depth and Complexity. (2022, March 10). *Depth and complexity resources and professional development.* J Taylor Education. https://www.jtayloreducation.com/.
+ Heacox, D., & Cash, R. (2019). *Differentiation for gifted learners: Going beyond the basics* (Revised and updated edition). Free Spirit Press.
+ Kettler, T., Lamb, K. N., & Mullet, D. R. (2018). *Developing creativity in the classroom: Learning and innovation for 21st-century schools.* Prufrock Press.
+ Mofield, E. (2023). *Vertical differentiation for gifted, advanced, and high-potential students: 25 strategies to stretch student thinking.* Routledge Press.
+ Mofield, E., & Phelps, V. (2020). *Collaboration, coteaching, and coaching in gifted education: Sharing strategies to support gifted learners.* Prufrock Press.
+ Roberts, J., & Inman, T. (2023). *Strategies for differentiating instruction: Best practices for the classroom* (4th ed.). Routledge.
+ Stambaugh, T., & Mofield, E. (2022). *A teacher's guide to curriculum design for gifted and advanced learners: Advanced content models for differentiating curriculum.* Routledge Press.
+ Winebrenner, S. & Brulles, D. (2018). *Teaching gifted kids in today's classroom: Strategies and techniques every teacher can use.* Free Spirit Press.

GT Toolkit of Models and Strategies

Acceleration/Enrichment Strategies		
What	**Why**	**How**
Acceleration	To progress in learning at a faster pace.	Students move at a faster pace or learn multiple standards at a time as they progress in a unit, content area, or grade level based on readiness levels.
Compacting	To progress in learning after content has been mastered	Students demonstrate mastery of content/standards (from a grade-level pretest or other form of assessment) and participate in alternative learning tasks (e.g., independent study, enrichment) instead of participating in learning activities related to content already mastered (Examples in Heacox & Cash, 2019; Winebrenner & Brulles, 2018).
Independent Study	To engage in research based on one's own interest	Students conduct independent research related to a topic or issue tied to their interest or content-area strength (eExamples Winebrenner & Brulles, 2018)
Tiering	To engage in learning tasks tied to readiness levels or interests	Students have opportunities to engage in learning tasks structured by various readiness levels or interests. Tasks can be tiered "up" by adding more advanced content, complexity, depth, abstractness, etc. (Examples in Roberts & Inman, 2023; Stambaugh & Mofield, 2022.)
Specific Instructional Strategies		
Analysis Wheels (Stambaugh & Mofield, 2022)	To analyze how parts of content relate; to apply complexity to learning tasks	Complexity is added to tasks requiring students to analyze how various elements of content relate to one another and interact. For example, students are asked to analyze the interaction of setting and character and how these interactions contribute to the theme. Analysis wheels are available in various content areas (e.g., STEM, Social Studies, rhetorical analysis, argument writing, etc.). (Examples in Stambaugh & Mofield, 2022.)

Acceleration/Enrichment Strategies		
What	**Why**	**How**
Concept Attainment (Bruner, 1973)	To analyze, to use critical thinking, and use inductive reasoning	Students are presented with an "unidentified" concept through keywords and phrases that have been classified into different categories (representing the concept). As the categories develop, students formulate their rationale for what they believe the concept is. Students then continue to test and refine their rationale until the concept has been successfully identified and synthesized through follow-up tasks. (Examples in Mofield & Phelps, 2020.)
Concept Development (Taba et al., 1971)	To use analysis and inductive reasoning	Students develop and support broad generalizations, rules, or predictions about a topic as a means to understand the big idea of what they are learning. Students sort concepts, identify categories, re-group the concepts with new categories, then develop a generalization based on patterns. (Examples in Mofield & Phelps, 2020.)
Connections to Big Ideas	To connect content to big ideas, generalizations, or principles; to make abstract connections	Add connections to universal themes/generalizations. For example, students connect their learning to a generalization such as "power is the ability to influence" in products, discussion, exit tickets, writing reflections, etc. (Examples in Stambaugh & Mofield, 2022.)
Depth and Complexity Thinking Tools (Kaplan, 2009)	To examine data and make connections within and across disciplines	These thinking tools can be used to guide students to examine content through the lens of a disciplinarian. Combine thinking prompts to add more depth and complexity to student tasks. Depth + Language of the discipline, Details, Patterns, Trends, Unanswered Questions, Ethics, Big Ideas Complexity + Change Over Time, Across Disciplines, Multiple Perspectives (Examples in Byrd & VanGemert, 2018.)

Acceleration/Enrichment Strategies		
What	**Why**	**How**
Double Fishbone	To analyze, cause-effect, identify underlying causes of problems, to forecast multiple implications	Students examine multiple causes (and causes of causes) and multiple effects (and effect of effects) of an issue. This allows for a more complex examination of content. (Examples in Mofield & Phelps, 2020.)
Metaphorical Expression	To use creative thinking; to make abstract connections	Students make abstract connections to classroom content by linking seemingly unrelated concepts together. Students' conceptual understanding is strengthened by connecting unfamiliar content to the familiar. (Examples in Mofield & Phelps, 2020; Mofield, 2023; Kettler et al., 2018.)
Mystery Box	To engage in inquiry, test hypotheses, make connections, arrive at conclusions	This inquiry-based activity presents students with riddles and/or artifacts that must be solved before moving forward in a unit of study. As students solve for unknowns, they gain a deeper understanding of key concepts, objectives, and content-specific generalizations. (Examples in Mofield & Phelps, 2020.)
SCAMPER (Eberle, 2008)	To use creative thinking/ divergent thinking	Students generate new ideas or improved ideas based on existing information. The following prompts are applied to a given idea- How might we . . .? + Substitute + Combine + Adapt + Modify (Magnify/Minimize) + Put to another use + Eliminate + Reverse/Rearrange (Examples in Cash, 2017; Mofield & Phelps, 2020.)

Acceleration/Enrichment Strategies		
What	**Why**	**How**
Six Thinking Hats (de Bono, 1985/2016)	To use critical thinking and creative thinking	Students examine and analyze information through six different perspectives including: + Facts (white hat) + Feelings (red hat) + Cautions (black hat) + Benefits (yellow hat) + Process (blue hat) + Creativity (green hat) (Examples in Kettler et al., 2018; Mofield & Phelps, 2020.)
Stretch Prompts (Mofield, 2023)	To use strategic thinking with support from scaffolds	These prompts can be used to increase the cognitive demands for student thinking with an aim to cultivate "thinking like an expert." These prompts include analyzing complex relationships, understanding patterns, applying criteria, constructing logical arguments, asking next step questions, transferring learning to new contexts, and being aware of one's own thought processes. (Examples in Mofield, 2023.)
RAFT (Santa et al., 2004)	To increase fluency, flexibility, originality, and elaboration in writing	Students choose a role as a writer (i.e. perspective), an audience, a format, and topic in order to write for different audiences. The varied formats allow for creative thinking and elaboration of the content.
Venn Diagrams +	To analyze relationships between multiple concepts	Beyond using a Venn Diagram to compare and contrast two concepts, a third or fourth concept (oval) can be added to increase the rigor of the task. Students research the concepts and determine the relationships among and between them. (Examples in Roberts & Inman, 2023.)
Thinking Models and Questioning Structures		
Bumping up Bloom's Taxonomy (Mofield, 2021)	To analyze, evaluate, or synthesize information with additional layers to extend learning.	Students are presented with more complex opportunities to engage with the upper levels (analyze, evaluate, create) of Bloom's taxonomy (1956) through the additional features of abstractness, critical thinking, complexity, and context. (Examples in Mofield & Phelps, 2020.)

Acceleration/Enrichment Strategies		
What	**Why**	**How**
Depth of Knowledge (Webb, 1997)	To use more sophisticated reasoning; to engage in deep learning; to transfer learning to new contexts	This model can be used to increase cognitive demands in learning tasks. + Depth of Knowledge 1: Recall/Reproduction: Builds foundation for deeper learning. + Depth of Knowledge 2: Application: Builds conceptual understanding. + Depth of Knowledge 3: Strategic Reasoning: Require reasoning and decision-making. + Depth of Knowledge 4: Extended Reasoning: Involves deep learning and transfer. (Examples in Mofield, 2023.)
Dimensions of Creative Thinking (Guilford, 1986/Torrance, 1962)	To use creative/divergent thinking	This model can be used to plan tasks using divergent thinking through the four dimensions of creativity: fluency (many ideas), flexibility (varied ideas), originality (new ideas), and elaboration (detailed ideas). (Examples in Cash, 2017; Kettler et al., 2018; Mofield & Phelps, 2020.)
Elements of Reasoning (Paul & Elder, 2019)	To use critical thinking; to construct logical arguments; to use analysis and evaluation	This critical thinking model can be used to enhance reasoning around issues or problems. The model includes the following components: + Purpose, Issue, Point of View, Assumptions, Evidence, Inference. Implications/Consequences, Concepts/Ideas The model can be applied to other strategies (6 Hats + elements of reasoning) and applied to advanced content.(Examples in Mofield, 2023; Mofield & Phelps, 2020; Stambaugh & Mofield, 2022.)

References

Bruner, J. S. (1973). Organization of early skilled action. *Child Development, 44*(1), 1–11 https://doi.org/10.2307/1127671.

Byrd, I., & VanGemert, L. (2019). *Gifted guild's guide to depth and complexity: Finding your way through the framework.* Gifted Guild.

de Bono, E. (1985/2016). *Six thinking hats.* Penguin. (Original work published 1985.)

Eberle, B. (2008). *Scamper: Creative games and activities for imagination development.* Prufrock Press.

Guilford, J. P. (1986). *Creative talents: Their nature, uses and development.* Bearly.

Kaplan, S. (2009). Layering differentiated curricula for the gifted and talented. In F. A. Karnes & S. M. Bean (Eds.), *Methods and materials for teaching the gifted* (3rd ed., pp. 107–156). Prufrock Press.

Kettler, T., Lamb, K. N., & Mullet, D. R. (2018). *Developing creativity in the classroom: Learning and innovation for 21st-century schools.* Prufrock Press.

Mofield, E. (2021). What makes honors classes more than a name? *AMLE Magazine.* https://www.amle.org/what-makes-honors-classes-more-than-a-name/.

Mofield, E. (2023). *Vertical differentiation for gifted, advanced, and high-potential students: 25 strategies to stretch student thinking.* Routledge Press.

Mofield, E., & Phelps, V. (2020). *Collaboration, coteaching, and coaching in gifted education: Sharing strategies to support gifted learners.* Prufrock Press.

Paul, R., & Elder, L. (2019). *Critical thinking: Tools for taking charge of your learning and your life* (3rd ed.). Pearson.

Santa, C., Havens, L. T., & Valdes, B. J. (2004). Project CRISS: Creating independence through student-owned strategies. Kendall/Hunt.

Stambaugh, T., & Mofield, E. (2022). *A teacher's guide to curriculum design for gifted and advanced learners: Advanced content models for differentiating curriculum.* Routledge Press.

Taba, H., Durkin, M. C., Fraenkel, J. R., & McNaughton, A. H. (1971). *A teacher's handbook to elementary social studies: An inductive approach* (2nd ed.). Addison-Wesley.

Torrance, E. P. (1962). *Guiding creative talent.* Prentice Hall.

VanTassel-Baska, J., & Baska, A. (2019). *Curriculum, planning, and instructional design for gifted learners* (3rd ed.). Routledge Press.

Appendix D

Differentiation Features to "Create the Challenge"

Feature	Meaning	Example Application
Complexity	Make connections among multiple ideas; observe inter-relationships between concepts; and understand multiple perspectives (Kaplan, 2009; VanTassel-Baska & Stambaugh, 2006).	Ask students to examine how the decreased bee population is the result of multiple factors and how it affects social, economic, and cultural systems.
Conceptual thinking	Link content to themes and big ideas (e.g., conflict, cycles, patterns, interactions, systems). Apply principles and theories.	Apply a concept such as "patterns" by asking, "How does the decrease in the bee population affect patterns within other systems (agricultural, economic, other species, etc.)?"
Creative thinking	Look at problems with new perspectives with an aim to create something new.	Develop multiple creative solutions for increasing the honeybee population and elaborating in detail how an original solution addresses the issue.

Feature	Meaning	Example Application
Critical thinking	Use reason and logic to analyze, evaluate, and construct arguments.	Critically analyze the pros, cons, biased perspectives, and effects of using pesticides and/or genetically modified crops.
Depth	Extend learning through examining trends, issues, and patterns within a discipline. Justify or construct a reasoned argument to develop a conclusion.	Pose a problem or issue (e.g., Should farmers continue to use pesticides to increase food yield?). Students construct and justify arguments with multiple sources.
High-level thinking	Analyze, evaluate, or synthesize information (from Bloom's taxonomy)	Students analyze multiple causes and effects of the bee population decreasing, evaluating effects on various points of view (farmers, environmentalists, consumers), and create an idea for an innovative form of technology to address the issue.
Open inquiry	Develop tasks with few parameters where students explore issues or problems.	Implement problem-based learning around the issue of the honeybee population decreasing. Students examine and define the problem and develop multiple solutions.
Posing boundaries	Make a task more challenging by posing set criteria and constraints within the task (Stambaugh, 2018).	Develop a proposal that includes ways for farmers to decrease the use of pesticides while also increasing food yield.
Transfer	Apply past learning to a new situation (real-world context)	Design a campaign to educate peers about protecting the bee population by describing the relationship between agricultural systems and ecosystems.

Adapted from Collaboration, Coteaching, and Coaching in Gifted Education: Sharing Strategies to Support Gifted Learners, Mofield, E., & Phelps, V. (2020), permission conveyed through Copyright Clearance Center, Inc.

About the Authors

Emily Mofield, EdD, is an Assistant Professor at Lipscomb University, Nashville, Tennessee, where she co-leads the graduate program in Gifted and Advanced Academics. Emily has over 20 years of experience in gifted education, recently serving as the NAGC Chair for Curriculum Studies. She has co-authored numerous NAGC award-winning advanced language arts curriculum units (with Tamra Stambaugh, Vanderbilt Programs for Talented Youth). She is also the author/co-author of several research publications and book chapters related to achievement motivation, collaborative teaching practices, and curriculum design. She is the co-recipient of the NAGC Hollingworth Award for Excellence in Research and 2019 Legacy Book Award for *Teaching Tenacity, Resilience, and a Drive for Excellence* (with Megan Parker Peters). She has also co-authored *Collaboration, Coaching, and Coteaching in Gifted Education* (2021 NAGC Book of the Year – Practitioner Category, with Vicki Phelps). She has most recently published two books featuring many tools and strategies for differentiation: *A Teacher's Guide to Curriculum Design for Gifted and Advanced Learners* (with Tamra Stambaugh) and *Vertical Differentiation for Gifted, Advanced, and High-Potential Students: 25 Strategies to Stretch Student Thinking.*

Emily regularly provides consultation and leads professional learning addressing collaborative teaching and use of differentiation strategies for advanced learners for school districts, conferences, and special groups. She also serves on the advisory board for the Javits Grant: Project BUMP UP on collaborative practices in gifted education. Emily is also the recipient of the Jo Patterson Service Award and Curriculum Award from the Tennessee Association for the Gifted, and the 2021 Dean's Award from the College of Education of Lipscomb University for significant contributions to the field of education.

Vicki Phelps, Ed.D., is Head of School for Quest Academy, a school for gifted learners, in Palatine, Illinois. She has been involved in gifted education for over 25 years, including teaching at both the elementary and secondary levels across Texas, Illinois, and Tennessee. She has served as an assistant professor, has collaboratively developed and opened a gifted magnet school, and enjoys providing professional learning and consultation services to school districts seeking to improve equitable gifted practices. In addition to being a featured guest on multiple webinars, podcasts, and social media chats, Dr. Phelps regularly presents at state, national, and international gifted conferences. She is the recipient of the 2021 NAGC Book of the Year Award - Practitioner Category (with Emily Mofield) for *Collaboration, Coteaching, and Coaching in Gifted Education*. In addition to her published research on gifted motivation and various other articles, her work is also included in *The New Teacher's Guide to Overcoming Common Challenges*. She is the author of *Successful Online Learning with Gifted Students* and *Strength-Based Goal Setting in Gifted Education: Addressing Social Emotional Awareness, Self-Advocacy, and Underachievement in Gifted Education* (with Karah Lewis). Dr. Phelps serves as the NAGC Chair for the Special Schools & Programs Network and enjoys reviewing manuscripts and proposals focused on gifted education.

For Product Safety Concerns and Information please contact our EU representative GPSR@taylorandfrancis.com Taylor & Francis Verlag GmbH, Kaufingerstraße 24, 80331 München, Germany